HOW TO

STYLE

your

BRAND

HOW TO

STYLE

your

BRAND

EVERYTHING YOU NEED TO KNOW TO
CREATE A DISTINCTIVE BRAND IDENTITY

FIONA HUMBERSTONE

COPPER BEECH

PRESS

For Pete, Ellie, Jasper
and Poppy, with love.

First published in 2015 by **Copper Beech Press**.
Reprinted in 2015.

Text copyright © 2015 Fiona Humberstone

The moral right of Fiona Humberstone to be identified as author
of this work has been asserted by her in accordance with the
Copyrights, Design and Patents Act 1988.

Editor: Joanna Copestick

ISBN 978 0 9564545 3 9

Printed in China

CONTENTS

CREATE YOUR LOGO 107

PULLING TOGETHER YOUR BRAND ELEMENTS 129

STYLING IT UP   181

RESOURCES 203

UNIQUE AND FANTASTICAL. This brand identity for Brazillian photographer Manuela Bertol encapsulates the spirit of brand styling. Each element is beautifully crafted, the design distinctive and energising and as a whole, the look striking and impactful.

INTRODUCTION

You're on the cusp of something big. Perhaps you're launching a new business or blog; maybe you're changing direction or, having run your business for several years, you're ready to up your game.

You understand that a smart, stylish and distinctive brand identity will get you noticed. You know that it'll help you attract the right sorts of clients and show the world how serious you are.

But how do you make sure that the time and money you invest in your branding will pay off? How do you make sure it'll be an accurate reflection of your aspirations and that it'll appeal to your most profitable clients, and more like them? How do you make sure you pick the right designer, brief them effectively and communicate your brand in a way that really represents you and your business?

You need a little focus, some insider knowledge and an experienced hand to guide you through the process.

And that's my goal for this book. I want to encourage you to think big about what's possible, to play to your strengths and achieve something utterly breathtaking.

CREATE A DISTINCTIVE BRAND IDENTITY

You'll discover how to go beyond creating a 'smart' face for your business and create something that has depth, emotion and style.

Smart just isn't good enough. Smart doesn't tug at the heartstrings or create a gut feeling. At best, smart reassures. But smart doesn't galvanise action; smart isn't compelling by itself.

This process is about creating something magical, something that creates an emotional connection between you, your business and your customer. It's about tapping into the overwhelming majority of customers who buy with their hearts, not their heads.

And, (whisper it), it's also about helping you fall back in love with your business. It's about inspiring you, letting you see the possibilities and getting out there to make things happen.

AN EXPERIENCED HAND TO GUIDE YOU

You can *so* create the right impression for your business: but you need a little know-how. And whether you're a startup looking for guidance on a lemonade budget or a seasoned entrepreneur determined to get your re-brand right, you'll find heaps of knowledge in this book to make sure that you create the very best impression you can.

No one teaches this stuff in business school (yet), but understanding how to either brief and evaluate creative work or create a powerful brand identity yourself is something every single entrepreneur needs to know.

This is the book I've always wanted to find for my brother-in-law, my best friend or the mum at the school gates who asks me: 'Where do I start?', 'How do I pick the right designer?' or, sadly, more often than not: 'Why don't I love what my designer has done and what should I do about it?'.

How to Style Your Brand will help you work out whether what's in your mind is right for your business. It'll walk you through the process of creating or commissioning something meaningful and long lasting from start to finish. And it'll be fun and hugely inspirational.

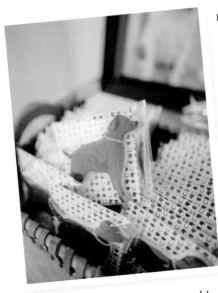

LUCKY, LUCKY LAB This creative and striking brand identity for Lucky Lab helped the mobile coffee bar launch with a splash. Turn to page 190 for the full story.

8

I'll share with you the secrets behind using colour to create an emotive connection; how to use pattern and illustrations to add character and personality and how to carefully select typefaces that add a distinctive and intentional edge to your designs.

We'll examine how to pull all of these elements together to create a remarkable and cohesive design that you can be proud of. I'll encourage you to think big about your business so that you develop the focus and vision to brief a designer with confidence, or to be able to create your own identity. Once you understand the principles behind styling a brand, there is no reason why you can't create something extraordinary for your business. I'll show you how.

Having developed hundreds of brand identities for companies across the world, I've seen first hand the impact that decent brand styling can have on a business. Not just in terms of the commercial success but also the energy and confidence that blossoms from an entrepreneur with a brand identity they can be proud of.

Now it's time to help you do the same for your business.

LIGHT AND BRIGHT London-based design blogger Geraldine Tan fills her workspace with colour and some of her favourite belongings. These fuel her creativity for her blog, Little Big Bell, while a pinboard makes it easy to switch up items as her inspirations change.

CHAPTER ONE

BRAND STYLING BASICS

"YOU DON'T NEED TO BE RICH TO SPARKLE."

WHAT IS BRAND STYLING?

Brand Styling is about bringing out the personality in your business with flair and intention.

It's about emphasising your best assets and creating a cohesive and compelling look. It's about telling a story, evoking the senses and captivating your clients. It's about aligning your identity with your business aspirations and helping you get to where you want to be, faster.

By carefully combining the right balance of colour, pattern, type, illustration and photography, you'll create a brand identity that's authentically and distinctively you.

I want to show you how to style a brand that reflects the very essence of your business and that helps you achieve your most ambitious of plans.

14

THE ART OF KEEPING Hannah Bergen offers a simple, low-tech, and lasting way for anyone to collect and document stories and information about a piece of furniture, art, tableware, or any sort of object. Framed photographs and wobbly candlestick holders each have stories — of travels, weddings, wars and loves. This exquisite brand identity was created by Stitch Design Co and helps Hannah Bergen clients to curate all the items needed to record and remember stories and memories associated with heirlooms.

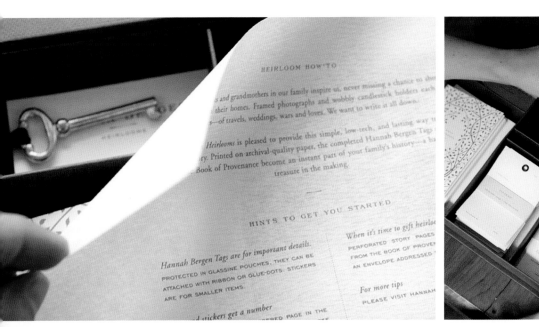

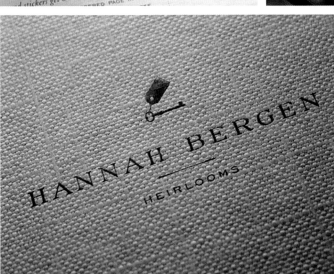

THE BRAND STYLING PROCESS

The best brand stylists know how to create something visually breathtaking, and more importantly, they know how to communicate with intention. They understand how to use colour to create an emotive connection, how to select fonts with just the right tone and personality, and how to add pattern, illustration icons and photography to add texture, depth and character. Throughout this book you'll find examples from small business owners and brand stylists who have done just that.

This workbook will walk you through the process of creating or commissioning an inspiring, creative and stylish brand identity that authentically reflects you and your business. From setting your vision to pulling together the detail, you'll find my expert tips and practical exercises ready to guide you, every step of the way.

Great design is nothing without focus and in this chapter, **Brand Styling Basics**, I'll explain how to start thinking about your own brand and how to take inspiration from everything around you. In Chapter Two, **Planning**, I'll encourage you to dig deep and think big as you define your intention for your business. This will form the foundations of a clear brief and will also serve as a key checking tool as you move on to the more creative elements of your journey. This focus will ensure that your newly styled brand really reflects you and your business, helping you to achieve your ambitions faster.

Armed with a sense of purpose from your planning, we then move on to creating a strong creative concept. In Chapter Three, **Create your Vision**, you'll research, brainstorm and mood board, as well as get acquainted with colour psychology. This

18

remarkable tool will enable you to create a cohesive brand identity that resonates with your target audience.

Your logo is perhaps the most prominent element within your brand identity and in Chapter Four, **Create your Logo**, we look at what it really takes to create a well-crafted logo. You'll be able to assess whether what you have right now is suitable for moving forwards, and if you need to adapt it, how to create a strong, professional-looking logo for your business.

You'll also need to incorporate colour, a range of fonts, perhaps illustrations, photography or pattern to add depth, character and individuality. In Chapter Five, **Pulling Together your Brand Elements**,

we'll combine all of these elements to build a strong brand identity. In Chapter Six, **Styling It Up** I share my top tips for creating a website that sells, a business card with impact and marketing literature that leaves a lasting impression.

This is a highly practical book that will demystify the design process and give you the confidence to take on branding your business with flair. Whether you need to undergo a complete transformation or a simple nip-tuck, I hope that you'll be inspired, empowered and well enough informed to get out there and create or commission the brand identity your business deserves.

THINK CREATIVE
An inspirational process for entrepreneurs, bloggers and freelancers

Whether you plan on following this process end to end yourself, or will work with a brand stylist, you'll find plenty of guidance and tried and tested advice to help you get the very best out of your project.

STYLE YOUR BRAND WITH FLAIR AND INTENTION

If you're someone who enjoys designing for your business you're probably comfortable finding your way around professional design programmes and will have a good understanding of design.

You've probably already created a smart logo or blog design and are ready to take things to the next level. I'll give you the tools to evaluate what you've already got and ensure that you communicate your business intentions through powerful design.

You'll find that the structured approach, the focus and objectivity you gain, combined with creative inspiration, will free you to create something utterly game changing and long lasting.

OUTSOURCE WITH
CONFIDENCE & CONVICTION

You may not wish to work on the actual design work yourself, but understanding how the creative process works, what to look out for and how to choose the right designer, is a skill every small business owner should have.

If you've ever felt the gut-wrenching disappointment of being underwhelmed by your graphic designer in the past, then you'll already understand the importance of getting yourself focused and choosing the right person to work with. This time things are going to be very different.

If you're determined to launch with a bang or get your rebrand right first time then you'll love the considered approach and hints and tips that'll guide you every step of the way.

CLEAR TIME AND SPACE FOR YOUR VERY BEST WORK

Styling your brand identity is a journey. It will stretch you, inspire you and unleash your inner creativity. It will challenge you to think big and stay focused.

At times it will be tough. You will need to think objectively and ask yourself some difficult questions about your business vision and what you are trying to do. But it will be worth it. There is nothing more rewarding than seeing all of your hard work come together: to create an identity that not only looks and feels fabulous, but most importantly, helps you achieve your business goals.

You'll need to set aside time to work through the exercises in the book, ideally half a day a week, more if possible. See this as a sound investment. It may be a cliché, but many of us simply don't work *on* our businesses enough.

Having spent seven years juggling a business and a young family I understand exactly how difficult it is to find the time, but find it you must, if you are to move forward. Just a few hours a week will make such a difference to your success, enabling you to create a strong business and follow through your goals.

23

MODERN HERITAGE Black and white, full of texture and rich with the sensibilities of the 1700's and today, this brand identity for Edmund's Oast was inspired by vintage newspaper rags and illustrated fables. Reclaimed wooden backers and a family of white and warm toned papers are the basis of a menu system that's flexible and easy to update on a daily basis.

HOW TO STYLE YOUR BRAND

YOUR BRAND IDENTITY SHOULD:

AUTHENTICALLY REPRESENT YOU AND YOUR BUSINESS. REFLECT YOUR VALUES & ASPIRATIONS. GIVE YOU CONFIDENCE. RESONATE WITH THE PEOPLE THAT MATTER THE MOST. BE DISTINCTIVE. SET YOU APART FROM YOUR COMPETITORS. HELP YOU GET TO WHERE YOU WANT TO BE, FASTER. BE UNIQUE. MAKE YOUR HEART SING & YOUR SPIRITS SOAR. EMBRACE THE POWER OF COLOUR. USE TYPE TO ADD CHARACTER & PERSONALITY.

nibs

download

THE BRAND STYLIST'S MANIFESTO

Styling a brand is about far more than creating a smart and professional 'look' for your business. It goes far deeper than that. Styling your brand well can help you achieve big things. Think of my Brand Stylist's Manifesto as a statement of intent, a call to arms if you like. Download a copy for your studio at **thebrand-stylist.com**

MAKING THIS WORK FOR YOU

I've structured this book in a way that broadly reflects the process I use to style a brand. That means that if you're coming at this with little, or no, design experience you might need to read through the whole book to gain an insight into some of the more technical elements like colour or typography before you can confidently tackle the creative work.

If you're an experienced designer you might find the creative work from Chapter Three, **Create Your Vision** onwards works better for you if you create colour palettes, illustrations and your logo designs concurrently, tweaking and refining as you go. I hope you'll find both approaches manageable and inspirational.

As you work through this book, be kind to yourself. Get into good habits that you'll want to keep up once this project is finished. Take yourself out of the office to your inspirational space and work through the exercises. Whether that's outside immersed in nature, surrounded by the buzz of your favourite café or on your sofa in your slippers, treat yourself to a bit of time and space. You'll be amazed how new ideas will start to flow.

Let's say goodbye to bland, apologetic and unimaginative branding and together let's create something that's impactful, distinctive and authentically you. Shall we get started?

THE ANATOMY OF A WELL-STYLED BRAND

A powerful brand identity is more than just the logo and a couple of colours, it's made up from a number of elements which add depth, texture and personality. And it's the sum of all of these parts that creates a brand identity that will really resonate.

JiLL SMiTH

COLOR PALETTE

PRIMARY ILLUSTRATIONS

SECONDARY ILLUSTRATIONS & ICONS

BRAND TYPOGRAPHY

GOTHAM   JiLL SMiTH PRO   KNOCKOUT

SECONDARY ILLUSTRATIONS & ICONS

TAGLINES

a design endeavor   *the MAgic of DESIGN*

Logo – of course! Think of your logo as the fullstop of your brand. It's instantly recognisable, it's distinctive but it doesn't need to tell your whole story – that's what the other elements are for.

A comprehensive **colour palette** that supports your brand messages.

Illustrations to add interest and personality.

A range of **typefaces** for body copy, headings, subheads and accents to enhance your brand identity and add character.

Devices and icons to add visual texture and further reinforce your brand. This might be an icon, a 'stamp' of some description or a set of illustrations.

Photography that adds an element of consistency and depth.

Brand **patterns** to add texture and flair. You'll use these perhaps on your website, your packaging or on the back of your business cards.

RAINBOW RAINDROPS Designer and letterer Jill Smith's brand identity is packed with personality. Quirky icons, off-the-wall illustrations and colourful patterns (including said rainbow raindrops) create a fun, witty and long-lasting impression.

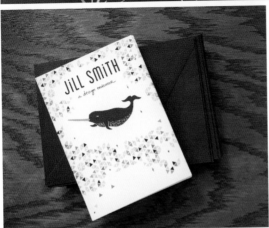

LEARNING FROM BRANDS YOU LOVE

Whether you're an experienced graphic designer or are completely new to this, you'll find your journey even more enjoyable and creatively rewarding the more inspiration you have at your fingertips.

Get into the habit of collating your inspirations online, perhaps via a blog or online scrapbook like Pinterest. More importantly, keep a visual journal of things that speak to you: clippings from magazines, patterns or fabrics that inspire you, colours that tug at your heartstrings or pieces of print that you just couldn't put down.

Think colour combinations, illustration styles, pattern, photography or favourite fonts. Think brand boards, like the one for Jill Smith on p26, logo designs, or web page layouts.

Notice who designed your favourites and start collating a list of designers whose work inspires you: we'll use it later when you come to selecting the right designer for your project. Look beyond Pinterest too: many top designers use websites Dribble and Behance to share their latest work. Start following your favourites and build up an inspiration library.

Look at some of the businesses whose branding you love, respect and admire. You may like to print out a screenshot of their website, or even brand board if it's something you've come across online. Perhaps you have some packaging or printed literature you can use? Paste everything into your journal and make some notes on what you see.

Make a point of asking yourself why something is working for you and what

28

specifically you like about it. Even when you see a piece of design that you love, if you look again you'll probably find that you're reacting to one or two key elements. Perhaps the colour, the typeface or a specific pattern or photograph. The more you can pinpoint precisely what you love, the more you'll be able to create something unique for your business.

Take some time to really dissect what you see. Which details inspire you? Ask yourself what you would change, or make your own, given the chance? You'll find that you can develop your own distinctive sense of style that reflects your unique business.

Inspiration is one thing, imitation quite another. We are aiming to style a brand identity that is unique to your business. And that means being aware of the inspiration that's around you, but also having the confidence to find your own style.

Throughout the book, you'll discover how to take your inspiration and turn it into something that feels unequivocally, definitively you. For now, simply keep your eyes open and look out for bright ideas.

CHAPTER TWO

PLANNING

"IT'S NOT HARD TO MAKE DECISIONS
ONCE YOU KNOW WHAT YOUR VALUES ARE."
-ROY E DISNEY

DEFINE YOUR INTENTION

Intention will make the difference between a superficially pretty brand identity and one that has traction. One that captures the essence of your business and wins you work.

It costs you nothing, other than your time, to sit down and really consider how your business should be perceived. And yet in my experience, most business owners just don't think hard enough or often enough about branding basics, such as who their most profitable clients are or what makes their company unique. Fewer still ensure that this knowledge is channelled through to the design of their brand identity.

For example, if you know you want your business to be seen as creative, inspirational and approachable, there are fonts and colours you can use which will communicate that. I'll show you exactly how to do this in the chapters that follow, but first we need to do some groundwork.

My approach to brand styling is about pulling together the elements that will drive your business forwards. It's not about being a slave to design fads or behaving like a magpie, it's about creating something utterly compelling.

In Planning you're going to think about what you want your business to be known for and how you want to be perceived. You'll consider your current and prospective clients, your space in the market and what you bring to the party. By the end of this process, you'll have a clear idea of exactly what your new brand identity needs to do for your business and you'll be ready to start on the creative work.

This is a great opportunity to really examine your business, warts and all, and gain a strong understanding of what really makes your company unique. Let's look at your strengths, your space in the market and your clients. Finally let's think about you. What do you bring to the table and how much of yourself should you put into the business?

So grab your notebook and spend some time pondering your answers to the following questions. Mind map, create spider charts, write copious notes and deliberate as much as you can.

You may feel that some of the questions ask you very similar things and this is because I want you to really put your business under the microscope and be very specific. You'll find this process will help you realise your full potential and step up your brand significantly.

1

WHAT MOTIVATED YOU TO STYLE OR RESTYLE YOUR BRAND?

It's important for you to identify upfront why you're doing this. Do you want to be taken more seriously in the market? Are you launching a new business, product or service and therefore want to make the right impact from the get-go?

Perhaps you've had a fabulous year and have decided to celebrate with a look that really does you justice? Maybe you are changing direction and need your brand identity to reflect that? Whatever your motivations, be clear from the outset.

2

WHAT'S YOUR AIM FOR THIS PROJECT?

How will you know the rebrand has been a success? What do you need it to do for you? Are there misconceptions about your business right now? Do people think you're cheaper than you are perhaps? Are you attracting the wrong sorts of clients?

Perhaps you're losing business because you've changed direction, so your communications need updating to reflect that. Maybe you're missing opportunities or you're simply not being taken seriously. Where possible, create a SMART goal (specific, measurable, achievable, relevant, timed) that you can measure your success against.

WHAT DO YOU DO?
WHAT DO YOU SPECIALISE IN?

This may seem like a ludicrously obvious question. Of course you know what you sell. You probably also know what your bestselling and most profitable services are too. But bear with me for a moment.

You may find that your product and service range has grown out of all control. That in your quest to grow your business you've expanded, expanded, expanded and are now left with a literal or virtual range of products that you just can't shift. You've lost your unique selling point, people are confused by what you stand for and you're struggling to see the wood for the trees.

Take a breath and use this time to really examine where you are right now and where you want to be headed. If you could be known for just one thing in your business, what would it be?

If you could wave a magic wand and change one thing about your business, what would that be?

Are you selling what inspires you? Are you known for products and services that have you leaping out of bed in the morning? And do they sell? Are there product lines or services you'd like to drop and others that you'd love to major in? This is your chance to gain focus or to reinvent yourself and your business!

WHAT MAKES YOU STAND HEAD AND SHOULDERS ABOVE THE COMPETITION?

When you're in the thick of running a business it can be easy to focus on the wrong things. The reason you didn't win a project. The apparent success your competitors are having right now. The client that didn't quite have the experience you set out to create.

Whilst it's important that you understand what's going on in the market and you listen to feedback, what's even more important is that you maintain your confidence and belief in what you're doing.

Your entrepreneurial vision, your style and your unswerving commitment to what you do are the greatest assets your business has: protect and celebrate them.

And so rather than focusing again on what you could be doing better and where you want to be headed next, let's look at what you're doing well right now. Take a moment or two to focus on the things that you do better than anyone else.

What do you really excel at? What else? And what else?

5 WHO ARE YOUR PROFITABLE CLIENTS? WHY DO THEY BUY FROM YOU?

Profitable clients are the ones who value what you do and are prepared to spend what you want to charge. They pay on time, they are happy to fit into the way that you work best and they love what you do. They recommend your business to equally wonderful people and they don't make unreasonable demands of you or your time.

They are the people you need to attract more of. So who are these profitable clients and what motivates them to work with you? What do they value about what you do?

It may sound obvious but having asked hundreds of business owners this very question, I promise you it's one that many of us don't think about often enough. Use this time as an opportunity to cherish the clients that you really want and attract more like them. Be brave.

6 IS THERE A TYPE OF CLIENT YOU'RE NOT CURRENTLY ATTRACTING?

You want more of your best clients, that's a given. But is there another group of customers who would really benefit from your business that you're not currently attracting?

Who would you really love as a client? Which blogs or magazines would you love to be associated with or featured in?

Could you put together a list of dream clients? Ask yourself: 'What would these prospective clients need to see on my website to be compelled to do business with me?'

FINDING HOME

Gather · Create · Connect

NEW YORK

COLOR PALETTE

FINDING HOME
LIFESTYLE BLOG & SUGAR MAKERS

Laura and Dana Putnam are quite literally, living their dream. After many years flying the corporate flag whilst wife Laura blogged about her inspirations at home, the Finding Home blog is now a sugar house, online shop and full-on family affair.

The family are now busy making a life and a living doing what they love best – crafting maple syrup and creating a welcoming home. Readers can shop for maple syrup along with home decor and holiday items.

This change in tack was the catalyst for the couple to commission a rebrand: a contemporary yet homely identity that could grow with the business.

Taking inspiration from Laura's grandfather and his love of cardinals, and the story of Noah's dove, Braizen created a visual representation of the spirit behind Finding Home – the spirit of family, warmth, and defining a space where those things come to life.

COLOR PALETTE	TYPOGRAPHY
	**BRANDON GROTESQUE** *P22 Franklin Caslon Italic* *Quickpen* CANTARELL

PATTERNS

ILLUSTRATIONS

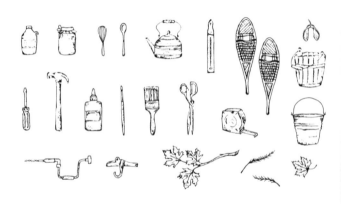

7 WHAT DO YOU FIND MOST INSPIRATIONAL ABOUT YOUR BUSINESS?

How often do you stop and think about what really inspires you about your business? The right brand identity can help you attract more of the clients and work that has you leaping out of bed in the morning — and less of the stuff that leaves you with that unpleasant knot in your stomach.

Is there anything that needs to change about the way you present your business so that you can do more of the things that you love and less of those that you don't?

Think about the kinds of clients that inspire you. Be specific. What, precisely, is it about that client that you admire? What is it about the project that motivates you? How can you tap into that energy to grow your business? Because the truth is that when we're happy, inspired and confident, we attract more of our profitable clients.

8 WHAT VALUES DRIVE YOUR BUSINESS?

This is quite possibly the most important question anyone in business needs to answer. Why do you do what you do? This is about the authenticity and the drive that keeps you going when things get tough.

You might find this question very simple to answer. Some of us are very conscious of both our personal and business values (which often overlap) and will be able to write down an answer in a matter of moments.

Some of you may find this question more of a challenge. If you struggle to answer it, I recommend you think about it differently and ask yourself: 'What's important to you about the way you run your business?' 'What matters in terms of how you treat your clients, staff and suppliers?'

9 WHAT DO YOU WANT TO BE KNOWN FOR?

All of the thinking you've done so far leads to one, simple question. What do you want to be known for? Let's bring together your understanding about your most profitable clients, your space in the market and what inspires you, to create an utterly compelling proposition. To be truly successful you need to stand out, be distinctive and create a business that's in a category of just one. Challenge yourself to dig deep and be brave.

If you were to plot out what makes you different from your competitors, how would that look? What proposition are your competitors trading on and how is that different from what you want to be known for?

Take into account any insider knowledge you've gleaned from mystery shops, feedback from clients and competitor research, as well as what they talk about on their website and in social media. How are you doing things differently?

What is it about your product or service that your clients really value? What makes you unique? And how can you communicate that through your new brand identity and in your marketing literature?

Find a spot in the market that only you can own and use this focus to align all of your communications with this one, compelling proposition. For instance, if you sell creative services, edit your portfolio down so it only shows the work that you want to win more of, the work of which you are overwhelmingly proud. This can be a bold move, but will pay dividends in the end.

You can't be all things to all people, so create a proposition so effective that it has clients crossing continents to work with you. It takes confidence to create this amount of focus, but by honing your product range or services to such a highly targeted style, proposition or offer, you'll make your business become irresistible.

10
WHO, EXACTLY, SHOULD THIS NEW BRAND IDENTITY BLOW AWAY?

Be honest with yourself here. Think broadly about who you really want to impress with your newly styled brand. Think beyond clients.

Perhaps there is a magazine editor or a blogger who you wish would take you seriously? Perhaps it's more about getting a big supplier or a retail outlet to take a closer look at your business? Maybe you wish to attract and retain quality staff? You're also going to be thinking about your most profitable clients too, of course...

Be as specific as you can. Think precisely about who within that list you want to wow and exactly what sort of thing is going to blow them away.

If you find that you're coming up with conflicting answers, now is the time to priortise, before you get yourself into a pickle trying to please everybody with your new design.

11
HOW SHOULD YOUR IDEAL CLIENTS FEEL WHEN THEY LOOK AT YOUR NEWLY STYLED BRAND?

Imagine way down the line when your beautifully styled new brand identity is on a new website or blog, or you hand a crisply printed business card over to an exciting new prospect. How should they feel? What should they think about your business?

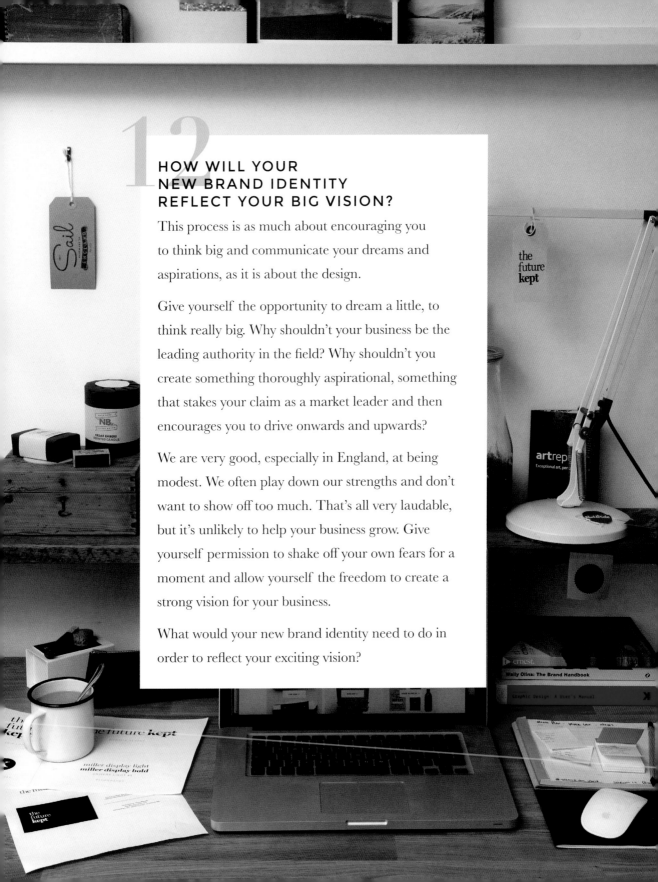

12

HOW WILL YOUR NEW BRAND IDENTITY REFLECT YOUR BIG VISION?

This process is as much about encouraging you to think big and communicate your dreams and aspirations, as it is about the design.

Give yourself the opportunity to dream a little, to think really big. Why shouldn't your business be the leading authority in the field? Why shouldn't you create something thoroughly aspirational, something that stakes your claim as a market leader and then encourages you to drive onwards and upwards?

We are very good, especially in England, at being modest. We often play down our strengths and don't want to show off too much. That's all very laudable, but it's unlikely to help your business grow. Give yourself permission to shake off your own fears for a moment and allow yourself the freedom to create a strong vision for your business.

What would your new brand identity need to do in order to reflect your exciting vision?

A QUESTION TO SET YOU FREE

Here's an emancipating thought: What would you be doing with your business if nothing were standing in your way? If you knew you couldn't fail? Who would you be working with, what would you be doing (or selling?) and how would you be doing it?

This can be an incredibly inspiring question. It encourages you to think bigger than you ever thought possible and create something that truly reflects you and your skills. And that can be terrifying and thrilling in equal measure!

45

"OUR DEEPEST FEAR IS NOT THAT WE ARE

INADEQUATE, BUT THAT WE ARE POWERFUL

BEYOND MEASURE."

- MARIANNE WILLIAMSON

Q&A

PRODUCE CANDLES
CHARLESTON, SOUTH CAROLINA

The story of Produce Candles is one of passion and curiosity. Farmers' market enthusiast Beau Burdette was so inspired by the diversity of produce available that she decided to distill it down into a range of hand-cultivated candles. Together with co-founder Adam Fetsch, she created a deliciously scented and unusual range that places striking design at the heart of the business.

With their sweet, earthy, spicy and crisp scents, each candle brings the best of the farm stall into the home. From names that include Beet, Kale, Wildflower and Melon, through to Carrot, Cilantro (Coriander) and Radish, Produce Candles brings a unique and fresh spin to a gift favourite.

This thoughtful and engaging brand identity, created by Stitch Design Co, comprises canning jars with silk-screened labels in patterns that represent each type of scent and produce. Each jar has a strong impact, singly and collectively.

Applied on top of each jar is a front and back label printed two colour and then embossed for that extra touch. The toppers are printed, laser die-cut and then embossed. Each topper is secured with a custom coloured rubber band (similar to those you see everyday in the produce section and farmers' market).

Rich, warm colours, natural textures and organic shapes create a truly exciting and memorable brand identity for this groundbreaking product.

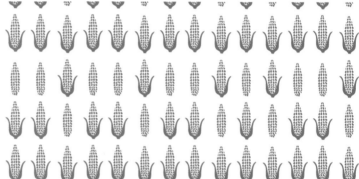

WHO ARE YOUR CUSTOMER ARCHETYPES?

When it comes to any type of creative work: writing copy, creating a brand identity or planning your website, you'll find the process infinitely easier if you are able to picture a specific person that you're communicating with, rather than a faceless 'audience'. Creating customer archetypes is one of the most powerful ways you can unlock your inspiration and create truly compelling work. Here's how to make it work for your business.

1 WHO IS YOUR MOST PROFITABLE OR LOYAL CLIENT GROUP?

Begin with your most profitable client and picture five or six key people within that segment so that you can understand them as fully as possible. Who is going to buy this range of products or services? What motivates them to buy? Why? Keep asking yourself why until you can't come up with any more answers.

2 WHAT DEFINES THIS CLIENT GROUP?

Give your archetype a name and really start to visualise them as a person. Write down as much as you know about any relevant personal information, such as their age, what they do for a living, family life and so on, and what they really value about your product or service. The more you can build up a picture here, the better.

3 WHAT TYPE OF BRANDING WOULD ATTRACT THIS CLIENT GROUP?

Start to tease out what brands they buy into, what magazines they read and where they shop. What do they aspire to and how does your business fit into this mix? Can you see how you can start to develop a brand identity that appeals directly to this type of customer?

MAKE A VISUAL REFERENCE THAT REFLECTS YOUR IDEAL CLIENT

Use catalogues, mailers, images you've sourced online, or perhaps images of your own, to create a visual reference that really reflects your ideal client. Use it to picture who you're talking to when you're writing your website copy or your email newsletters, as well as for this brand styling project.

Add logos from the brands your clients buy into, as well as magazine or blog logos, to build up the picture. This process almost always gets the creative juices flowing and will help you to start visualising the possibilities.

TIPS FOR SUCCESS

This exercise works really well if your business sells to consumers. It's slightly harder to do if you sell to other businesses, but it's worth trying to make it work. Remember, your business clients are people too!

If you sell a wide range of products, try segmenting them into the type of client that buys them and what motivates them to do so. Create one board for each product segment. Alternatively, you may like to create one board for each archetype.

If you're a blogger and you don't have customers, then this works just as well if you think about your most loyal readers — the ones that show up regularly, always comment on your posts and often share your content with their followers.

50

PULLING TOGETHER A FOCUSED BRIEF

When you design for yourself it's very tempting to skip the creation of a written brief and instead jump straight onto your computer and start designing. This can lead you to lose focus quite quickly though. Writing out a formal brief for yourself may feel a bit bureaucratic, but it's the best way to formulate your ideas and will prevent you from behaving like a magpie, getting distracted by all the many things that you want to incorporate (some relevant, many not).

Without a proper brief you can easily forget what it was you set out to achieve. Something that should have taken a few weeks, from start to finish, could then quite possibly take more like six months.

Worse still, if lacking in direction, you start to search for reasons to justify the design decisions you've made. Yes it looks lovely, but is it saying the right things about your business?

So, if you're tempted to miss out this section and move onto the fun stuff, allow me to encourage you to take time to get properly focused and document what's in your head. A concise brief will ensure you'll always have something to refer back to, and it will provide the objectivity and clarity you will need later.

"SHE TURNED HER CAN'TS INTO CANS

AND HER DREAMS INTO PLANS."

- KOBI YAMADA

CREATING YOUR BRIEF

By now you will have gathered lots of notes, created spider diagrams and generally dug deep, thanks to the work we did in the first section of this chapter. The next step is very simple: you just need to transpose this to a concise brief that you can refer back to as you work through the design process.

You can download an example of the brief I use at **thebrand-stylist.com**. Simply print it out and fill in the blanks.

You'll notice that I've added a couple of extra sections to my brief. Firstly I ask you to write down sites and brands that inspire you – leave that bit for now, we will come to that next. Secondly I'm asking you to be bold – write down three key words that sum up what you want your brand to be. This is so important.

The truth is that when you're designing a new brand identity you can't make it tick fifteen boxes: you'll end up with a watered down, muddled and messy design that appeals to no one. But three? Yes, three is very achievable. So be strong and focused.

Are you finding it tricky to narrow it down? It can be difficult when you're so close to something, but I find it helps to think about things laterally. Many of the words you've written down will probably relate to each other. So, if there are words you really can't give up on, ask yourself: Is the meaning of one of the words encapsulated by others you won't let go of? Can you group them together in one 'umbrella' word instead?

For example, you may want your new brand identity to have clarity. Perhaps you also want it to be clean, smart and distinctive. All of those words can be grouped together without watering down what you're trying to achieve. In fact, by grouping the words together you're starting to get a much stronger idea of what *you* actually mean by clarity.

Armed with your top three words (not to mention your inner peace at having documented a jumble of inventive thoughts into something much more ordered and manageable), let's move on to the first creative process: The Big Vision.

52

"IT'S NOT WHAT YOU ARE THAT HOLDS YOU BACK,

IT'S WHAT YOU THINK YOU'RE NOT."

- DENIS WAITLEY

the
download

CHAPTER THREE

CREATE YOUR VISION

"IF YOUR DREAMS DON'T SCARE YOU,
THEY'RE NOT BIG ENOUGH."

This is quite possibly the most inspirational, creative and fun element of the whole brand styling process. This is your opportunity to think big, be brave and be bold. It's your chance to see beyond what's already out there and create something truly unique. In this chapter you'll discover how to pull together your influences and inspirations into a concept that authentically reflects your business.

You'll research, brainstorm and mood board as well as learn about colour psychology, which is going to be game-changing.

As we progress, you'll gradually gain a clear idea of how your brand should look and feel. Once that's done, you'll then be ready to start the design process.

GETTING INSPIRED BY WHAT'S POSSIBLE

Let's start with a little research. We're working towards creating a vision board for your brand that will set the tone and visual aim for your new brand identity. The first step is to be inspired by what's possible.

This stage is about gathering thoughts and looking for things that will spark off ideas in your mind. It's about getting into your creative zone, working out what you love and why. Remember that to create a truly powerful brand you must create something unique. So, resist the temptation to replicate some, or all, of what you see. Ask yourself why you're responding to something and how you might make it your own.

Now is the time to pull out your scrapbook.

You're going to find this exercise much easier if you're the sort of person who keeps their eyes open at all times and really notices things such as changing window displays in your local town centre or shopping mall; catalogues and direct mailers that

come through the post; packaging for the goods that you buy. All are rich sources of inspiration for the aspiring brand stylist.

Make use of websites like Pinterest and Behance. Visit blogs which showcase great design work and get into the habit of asking yourself: 'Why do I like this?' 'How is this relevant to what I do?' 'How would I make this my own?' It's that last question that really matters. Good design is about inspiration not imitation, and the more you can make something your own, then the better your design, and your business, will be.

Keep tear sheets from magazines, print off work that particularly inspires you and get into the practice of making notes. The best brand stylists don't slavishly copy, they don't recreate something that's worked for another company; they understand the trends, the essence of what's going on in a market and they work out how to create something that answers the brief of their client.

LOOK AT YOUR COMPETITORS

Let's start by looking at how your competitors are currently marketing themselves. Visit their website, print out a screenshot if you see something you like and stick it into a scrapbook along with some notes on what you see.

You know how you want your business to come across from the work we did in Planning. What messages are your competitors communicating and how successfully are they doing so? What is working for them and what isn't? Are you inspired by anything you see?

If you've created yourself a truly unique space in the market, then you won't be sending out the same signals as your competitors. But it's still worth taking an objective analysis of their website and brand identity. What have they done well? What message do they communicate through their choice of fonts, colours and imagery?

Does anything that you see make you think differently about your brief? Tweak it if you need to, but only once you've reflected on

your changes – the reason you've written down your brief is to avoid confusion once you start researching.

Think beyond your local competitors. What are the market leaders doing and what can you learn from them? Look overseas too, how are people in your industry branding themselves internationally? Does anything you see inspire you or encourage you to think even bigger than you thought possible?

COMPARISON IS
THE THIEF OF JOY

Whilst it's important you understand what your competitors are up to, I'm not suggesting that you start continually checking their social media feeds on a daily or even weekly basis. Following your competitors' every move is bad for morale and it's bad for your business. It can harm your confidence and distract you from what really matters.

Set your own pace, follow your own inspirations and pour your energies into your own vision.

WHO INSPIRES YOU?

Now, let's think a bit more laterally. Which businesses inspire you? And what can you learn from your response to their design? As always, ask yourself: 'What, specifically, do I like about this' and 'How would I make this my own?' Make copious notes, sketch out ideas and fill your head with possibilities.

You might look at businesses that service the same clients as you, but sell something totally different. For example if you were a garden designer with a particularly contemporary style, you might look at architects, interior designers and homeware brands that share your aesthetic.

It's hard to tell you how to search for this sort of thing online because it's a knowledge that you'll build over time. You might simply start looking for inspiration on some favourite blogs or Pinterest and see where that leads. Not everything will inspire you, but there will be some gems that help your understanding of how your brand might be.

Finally, it's also worth exploring magazines, catalogues, blogs and websites that simply inspire you on a general level. They may have nothing to do with your business whatsoever, but for some reason you're drawn to them. Why is that? What fonts, colours and design devices do they use? And is there anything in this that could work for your business? As before, print out screenshots and make notes of any ideas that come to mind.

At the end of this process my hope is that you'll be feeling inspired and excited by the possibilities. You may also be feeling a little confused. You have so many ideas, often conflicting in style, that it's hard to see how you're going to pull them together into a coherent vision. Fear not, we will get there! And colour psychology is going to play a big part in that.

COLOUR PSYCHOLOGY

Your secret weapon!

Have you noticed how experienced designers seem to be able to pull together designs effortlessly? Things just seem to 'work' and it can be hard to see how or why?

What you learn from colour psychology will enable you to understand exactly why things work, and conversely, what to change when a design isn't coming together.

Colour psychology will provide the insights, guidance and structure to efficiently create a coherent design. It will give you the confidence that what you are doing will work at a practical level, as well as creating that all-important emotive and instinctive reaction. Remember it is this reaction that compels people to buy into you and importantly, buy from you.

We all see colour differently, but once you start to understand how certain personality types respond to colour, you can use this to your advantage.

Colour works at a subconscious level, faster than words or images, and creates a gut response. By understanding how colour psychology works, you can style a brand identity that feels as good as it looks.

You're going to start by identifying which of the four seasons your business falls into and that will determine the tones of colour, shapes, fonts even patterns you choose. Later in the book I'll show you how to use this seasonal personality to guide your choice of supporting brand elements, but for now we are all about the vision.

62

THE SEASONS

There are four main seasons with very distinctive personalities that provide the basis for selecting colour, texture, pattern and other brand styling elements. As I introduce each season I suspect that certain seasons may have more resonance with you than others – this is a good thing! Notice which you're most drawn to as we work through each one.

In order to create a cohesive brand you've got to commit to one season with, at most, one subordinate season. You'll notice that each season, and each colour, has positive and negative qualities to it. Stick to one season and you'll find that you communicate the positive qualities of the season and avoid any potential negative connotations.

You'll notice that each season is very 'people' driven. Effectively what we're doing here is capturing the personality of your business and, where appropriate, the personality of the owner behind the business.

The seasons are very much rooted in what happens in the natural world throughout the year and there is a real flow between the season and the personality, just as between the business and the personality type. As you read, consider your own experiences of each season. What resonates with you the most? And which do you feel represents your business in the way you'd like to be seen?

THE SPRING PERSONALITY

The first signs of spring are enough to fill many of us with an optimism and energy that is just the tonic after a long winter. Think trees laden with delicate blossom in pretty pastel tones, or verdant green shoots from plants awakening from dormancy, filling us with hope and optimism for the year ahead. And just as the spring bulbs and plants burst through the barren winter soil with their promise of life and exuberant colours, so spring people light up a room with their expressiveness, their creativity and inspirational ideas.

Infectiously enthusiastic, incredibly bright and very people-focused, spring personalities are big on fun. They are excellent communicators, good at thinking on their feet and brimming with ideas. Clarity, simplicity and transparency is important to them.

Spring personalities multi-task well and love working with people, bouncing ideas around and bringing teams together. They are social animals and they love to entertain. They think creatively and quickly – often their heads are literally spilling over with ideas – and are a real inspiration to those around them. Their challenge is to hold themselves back and ask themselves exactly which of their latest fabulous ideas they should focus on.

The flipside to all this energy is that it can often be hard to contain a spring personality. They flit from one idea to another, leaving a trail of unfinished projects in their wake. Others may see them as flaky, unreliable and less serious than they really are. They can be perceived as downmarket, and their youthful looks don't always work in their favour.

KEY SPRING ATTRIBUTES

Clarity, simplicity, sparkling, forward thinking, creativity, open, communicative, bursting with life, bubbly, on trend, contemporary, quick thinking, friendly, optimistic.

ONE ELEVEN

COLOR PALETTE

No. 111

BRAND ICON

SECONDARY LOGOS / WATERMARKS

WHIMSICAL AND CLEAN This beautiful brand identity for Californian family and lifestyle photographers One Eleven helps owner Jenna Elliot stand out in a highly saturated market. Taking their inspiration from her star sign (Capricorn) and her love of all things vintage and pretty, Braizen have created a knockout brand identity that's fun, professional and timeless.

TYPOGRAPHIC ACCENTS

XO *Jenna*   *So Cal*   *No.* 111   THE *Elliotts*

BY *Jenna Elliott*   WEDDINGS *And* FAMILIES

A Sign of Good Times   *Signs of Truth & Beauty*

TYPOGRAPHY

TREND SANS   Cantarell   *Rolling Pen Complete*

PATTERNS & TEXTURES

SPRING AT A GLANCE

Fun, youthful, forward-thinking, creative, inspirational, expressive, clarity, approachable, excellent communicators.

COLOURS

Light, bright and clear – from the bright warmth of the spring bulbs to the pastels of the spring blossoms. Think primrose yellow or verdant lime green.

SHAPES, FONTS, TEXTURES

Circles, polka dots, ditsy, busy patterns. Fonts with clarity and rounded shapes. Clean and glossy textures. Glints and sparkles. Fine lines. Anything with the appearance of movement.

TYPICAL SPRING BUSINESSES

Creative and communications-based industries: marketing, PR, digital and creative agencies, photographers. Those with a youthful approach to business: children's party entertainers, children's clothes designers, nurseries.

THE SUMMER PERSONALITY

As summer temperatures soar, so colours fade and take on a more delicate, muted tone. Think hazy, lazy summer days by the beach or lake and long, lingering evenings sharing supper outside with friends and family.

The pace in summer is altogether more considered, measured even, and the manic energy that spring brought with her has faded. Do we achieve less in summer? Absolutely not, but summer personalities are less inclined to jump up and down and tell the world constantly about their every move.

Often graceful, elegant and stylish, quality is key to the summer personality. With a strongly intuitive and romantic side, many summer businesses have strong links to the wedding industry. From florists, photographers and dress designers to planners and stylists, their understated style, creativity, commitment to quality, luxury and style make a perfect match for brides.

Summer personalities are efficient, productive and well-organised. Detail is everything and they leave no stone unturned in their quest for perfection. They thrive on structure, order and process and they dislike the rapid change that their more spontaneous counterparts love to throw at them.

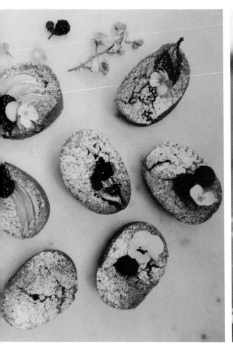

Summer personalities tend to be reserved, in sharing their opinion, they are much more likely to observe a situation and hold back on their thoughts until asked. This can sometimes lead others to see them as a walk over: don't be fooled! They know their own minds and are much more resilient than you give them credit for.

Negatively, summer personalities can sometimes seem to lack spontaneity, which can be frustrating to those around them. They seldom show their emotions and their naturally reserved nature can be seen as stand-offish, aloof even, and sometimes too

KEY SUMMER ATTRIBUTES

Elegant, romantic, graceful, reserved, efficient, balance, proportion, harmony, abstract, misty, dreamy, luxurious, quality, aspirational.

formal. Their drive for perfection can hold them back, but they will always be realistic about how long a task will take and what is required to complete it: in short, you can rely on summer. They are very supportive, sensitive to the feelings of others and have a strong sense of responsibility.

SUBMARK   HAND DRAWN ELEMENTS   SUBMARK

72

COLOR PALETTE

**TRADITIONALLY
CRAFTED** Rona Wheeldon
is a flower writer, presenter
and blogger at Flowerona.
Having recently launched
a new range of business
workshops for florists, and
started to make her dream
of becoming a TV presenter
reality, Rona approached
Salted Ink to create a new
brand identity that reflected
her business aspirations.
The new design perfectly
encapsulates the beautiful
and inspirational nature of
her blog. A deep eggplant
tone adds weight to a soft
summer palette and shows
the world just how serious
Rona is about her business.

FONT SUGGESTIONS

magallanes essential light
ABCDEFGHIJKLMNOPQRSTUVWXYZ
abcdefghijklmnopqrstuvwxyz

NEVIS BOLD
ABCDEFGHIJKLMNOPQRSTUVWXYZ
abcdefghijklmnopqrstuvwxyz

PATTERNS AND TEXTURES

SUMMER AT A GLANCE

Organised, logical, efficient, intuitive, empathetic, creative, graceful, elegant, aspirational, chic, understated, strong sense of responsibility.

COLOURS

Cool, delicate and muted. Think lavender and English roses as well as old school, establishment colours such as navy blue or British racing green.

SHAPES, FONTS, TEXTURES

Flowing, elegant lines, delicate florals, beautiful script fonts and traditional serif fonts with grace. Watercolours, faded florals, soft vintage styling. Quality is essential to the summer personality, so beautifully textured paper or fabric – anything as long as it's not cheap!

TYPICAL SUMMER BUSINESSES

Creative professionals: interior, graphic and jewellery designers. Wedding planners, photographers, classical musicians. Quality, well established and serious businesses: lawyers, accountants.

THE AUTUMN PERSONALITY

Autumn: season of mists and mellow fruitfulness. The garden is at it's bountiful peak, flowers are getting ready for their last hurrah and there is a feeling of exuberance and productivity. Colours are bold, intense, muted and very beautiful.

Leaves turn intense shades of red, copper, gold and yellow before fluttering to the ground and leaving a very different landscape at the end of the season to the one we started with. The gentle pace of summer is over: autumn runs at a pace.

Passionate, energetic, enthusiastic and highly independent, autumnal personalites love to challenge established norms. They are great campaigners and have a strong sense of justice.

Warm, friendly, loyal and earthy people, they have a great love and respect for the natural world.

Just like the spring personality, they too often take on too much – but their organisation, practicality and strong work ethic means that they will rarely let you down.

Substance, authenticity and integrity is hugely important to them. And whilst family and friends are at the heart of the autumn personality, so too is personal achievement. They are lifelong learners and their professional status is important to them. Balancing these two strong values can often be a source of stress for the autumn personality.

They find it difficult to see things from others' perspectives and can be stubborn when challenged. They find it hard to let go and often hold on to baggage for far too long both literally and emotionally. They can be bossy, rebellious, temperamental and unpredictable - exhausting those around them!

The autumnal personality loves the past and is often fascinated by history. Dusty books, academia and nostalgia are also key. They are collectors, sometimes obsessively so. Expect to walk into their home and be greeted by hundreds of cookbooks, or Penguin Classics or vintage records: whatever their passion should be, rest assured that they will pursue it with vigour.

KEY AUTUMN ATTRIBUTES

Passionate, warm, energetic, ambitious, earthy, organic, authentic, abundant, cosy, comfortable, family, lifelong learners, history.

ARTHUR COTTAM

· HORSESHOES ·

76

TRADITIONALLY CRAFTED This contemporary identity for family business Arthur Cottam draws on 90 years of family heritage and a strong tradition of craftsmanship. As you would expect of a business so connected to the outdoors, family and artisanship, this is primarily an autumn brand but the palette pulls in the softer, almost summery tones which keeps things traditional and highly aspirational.

ARTHUR COTTAM
· SOUTHWEST ·

ARTHUR COTTAM
· HEATHFIELD ·

EQUI-SHOE
· DESIGNED BY ARTHUR COTTAM ·

VANTAGE
· TOOLS ·

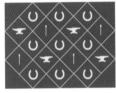
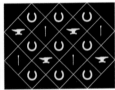

AUTUMN AT A GLANCE

Ambitious, focused, nature, earthy, organic, strong connection with the outdoors, integrity, strong sense of history, substance, authenticity, challengers, campaigners.

COLOURS

Warm, intense and muted. Think turning leaves and the colours of harvest. Of all the seasons, autumn has the widest gamut of colours, from burnt umber to pale straw.

SHAPES, FONTS, TEXTURES

Squares with rounded corners, pattern with natural texture and substance, slightly informal illustrative styles with substance. Acrylic or gouache paints, chunky header fonts and natural hand-rendered fonts for approachability. Natural textures and preferably recycled or textured paper.

TYPICAL AUTUMN BUSINESSES

Research, journalism, psychology, archaeology or history. Organic or fairtrade businesses, outdoors, animal, community or charity.

THE WINTER PERSONALITY

From the clear, sparkling light of the sun catching frosted seed heads to the dull, drizzly, depressing days that seem to go on and on, winter is a season of extremes.

The winter personality is realistic, self assured, practical and reliable. They are grounded, intelligent and ambitious people who make things happen with the minimum of fuss.

Winter personalities make for highly driven, successful and decisive business owners. They have the ability to both create the big vision and drop down to the detail. They are focused, objective and detached. They get things done and they get them done now.

It'll be no surprise then, to find that typical winter businesses include technology companies, digital agencies and financial services. Luxury goods such as jewellery, high-end travel companies and many fashion labels sit comfortably within this season.

Winter is glamorous, opulent, luxurious, rich, even. Conversely it's also understated, grounded and unfussy.

Naturally this focus and objectivity brings with it certain challenges. Winter personalities can sometimes be seen as being cold, uncaring and insensitive. Their ambition can be alienating to those around them and they need to consider how they

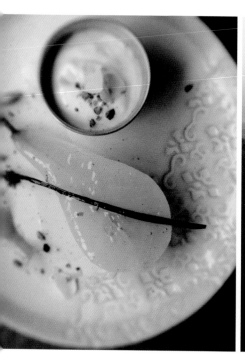

communicate with those less on their wavelength. The winter personality tells it like it is, and they don't suffer fools gladly.

It's important to note that the winter palette is the only one that contains black. Sitting comfortably within this season, black exudes luxury, style and success, mixed into other seasons it can make your brand look downmarket, unimaginative and lacking in style.

KEY WINTER ATTRIBUTES

Strong, dynamic, dramatic, focused, uncompromising, luxurious, opulent, lavish, glamorous, theatrical, decisive, expert, grounded, practical.

APPROACHABLE LUXURY Julie, the founder of
Olivine has been dreaming up fragrances and cosmetics
to help women feel more beautiful for over 20 years.
Her sophisticated and timeless brand identity can grow
with the business as they introduce more product
lines. Kraft boxes and thick, matte labels keep the line
luxurious yet approachable and a piece of gold-flecked
baker's twine adds the perfect finishing touch. The
feather device references the gold-dipped feathers
tucked inside the packaging.

WINTER AT A GLANCE

Decisive, driven, opulent, luxurious, self-assured, cutting edge, visionary, grounded.

COLOURS

Cool, strong, intense and clear. Think ice blue, sparkling metallics and neon tones. Note: this is the only season which contains pure black and white.

SHAPES, FONTS, TEXTURES

Geometric shapes, strong, clean patterns. Clean, strong, minimal fonts or highly opulent.

TYPICAL WINTER BUSINESSES

High-end jewellery and fashion, luxury travel, retail, cars and white goods. Banking, technology, finance and law. Also no-frills businesses, such as cheap holidays or flights.

FINDING THE SEASON THAT BEST REFLECTS YOUR BUSINESS

Understanding which season your business falls into is absolutely essential if you're to use colour psychology to its full potential.

Defining your seasonal personality helps you think big about how to style your brand. It gives you cues as to what fonts, patterns, textures and shapes will be right for your business and how best to communicate your brand values. It'll help you communicate with flair and intention and create something cohesive and long-lasting.

One of the challenges you'll find as you work through this process, is how far your personality should come into the brand. It's worth making a conscious decision at the start of the process about how interlinked your personality is with that of your business.

On page 85 you'll find a checklist that will help you really analyse the season that's right for your business based on your brief. By getting you focused before you start the creative work, we can balance your commercial objectives with the energy and passion you bring to the table and create an authentic and meaningful brand identity.

Remember, as long as you root your colour palette in your dominant season, you can pull in elements from your subordinate season to create a unique and balanced identity.

82

UNCOMMON ATTENTION TO DETAIL

A pared back colour palette, natural textures and understated, clean design keeps this brand identity for lifestyle and accessories store Commonplace, very much on the grounded side of winter. As carriers of premium leather goods, this authentic and highly compelling look appeals directly to their young, hip client base.

GOING BACK TO THE BRIEF

You've probably found that just by reading through the descriptions of each season you started to get a hunch for how your own business fits into the personalities? Perhaps it straddles a couple? That's OK too, but you will need to decide which is your primary season and then we can look at how we bring in elements of another season later.

The best way to do this is visually. So grab your brief and using a marker pen or set of coloured pencils start to highlight the words in your notes you think relate to each season. If you use a different colour for each season it'll be fairly easy for you to start to tally up which season is predominating.

Hopefully, from reading the descriptions, you'll have a strong idea about which words fit into which season. Opposite is a glossary of words to help you. You may not have outlined my specific phrases or words, but you should be able to make a best guess. Combine your own gut feel with a tally from the other words. You will then be able to finish this exercise with a confident sense of which season your business falls into.

Resist the temptation to work down the words opposite like a shopping list, ticking everything you think sounds good. Instead work methodically through the words you've already written down.

As a sense check, go back to your three most important words and you'll probably find that at least two out of the three are within one season. If you find all three are across the seasons and that the rest of your words are straddling the seasons equally then you need to go back and get focused! You simply cannot be everything to everyone. Rationalise your brief down to what really matters.

COLOUR PSYCHOLOGY KEYWORDS

SPRING	SUMMER	AUTUMN	WINTER
approachable	*aspirational*	*abundant*	*compelling*
bright	*attention to detail*	*ambitious*	*cutting edge*
brilliant	*balanced*	*authentic*	*decisive*
bubbly	*beautiful*	*campaigner*	*disciplined*
clear	*calm*	*comforting*	*distinctive*
clever	*creative*	*community*	*dramatic*
communicative	*dependable*	*earthy*	*driven*
creative	*efficient*	*efficient*	*expensive*
effervescent	*elegant*	*energetic*	*expert*
enthusiastic	*ethereal*	*enthusiastic*	*focused*
expressive	*flowing*	*environment*	*grounded*
fine	*gentle*	*evocative*	*hedonistic*
forward thinking	*graceful*	*exuberant*	*high achiever*
friendly	*intuitive*	*fiery*	*high end*
fun	*logical*	*flamboyant*	*luxurious*
imaginative	*nurturing*	*focused*	*market leader*
improviser	*organised*	*friendly*	*objective*
impulsive	*perceptive*	*growth*	*opululent*
informal	*perfectionist*	*hearty*	*practical*
inspirational	*precise*	*historic*	*precise*
light	*professional*	*independent*	*realistic*
lively	*quality*	*integrity*	*reliable*
open	*quiet*	*intense*	*self assured*
optimistic	*reliable*	*justice*	*serious*
personable	*responsible*	*learning*	*simple*
positive	*romantic*	*nature*	*single minded*
quick thinking	*sensitive*	*nostalgic*	*specialist*
simple	*serious*	*organic*	*stand out*
sociable	*soft*	*passionate*	*strong*
sparkling	*soothing*	*practical*	*uncompromising*
spontaneous	*supportive*	*productive*	*understated*
twinkly	*timeless*	*strong*	*unfussy*
warm	*traditional*	*substantial*	*visionary*
welcoming	*understated*	*unusual*	
youthful		*warm*	

MIXING SEASONS TO REFLECT YOUR UNIQUE BUSINESS

It's rare that a business will be clearly one season or another and this is how it should be. Your business is unique and it's important that you communicate that. More often than not you'll find that your business attributes fall across more than one season, so how do you tackle this?

Looking at your notes, you'll probably find that one season is particularly dominant but that there is most likely a subordinate season. I've always described seasonal personalities in terms of sides.

For example your business might be the spring side of summer – meaning that you have all the elegance, grace and romanticism of summer, but with the lightness, sociability and creativity of spring. So, you might use the softer, lighter tones of summer with some of the clarity and roundness of shapes that come with spring.

This can be a confusing concept if you're just learning about colour psychology, as we're using seasonal names but really talking about personalities and attributes. So it's perfectly possible to have a summer-side-of-winter personality when in nature there can of course be no such thing! Summer-side-of-winter would capture all of the luxury, elegance and style of winter, but with a softness that comes from summer. You'd use colours that have clarity to them but would probably avoid black, instead opting for a charcoal grey and perhaps a blush pink?

What's important is that you decide on your dominant season. That's going to determine the tones of colours you use. This is non negotiable. Do not mix tones of colours from one season with another, or you will end up with a horrid and unsettling mess. You'll undermine your credibility and get the wrong sort of emotive reaction.

86

Once you are clear on your dominant season, you can then use the styles from your subordinate season to create something that really captures the essence of your business.

Remember: spring colours are light, bright and clear; summer tones are cool, delicate and muted; autumn colours are warm, intense and muted and winter's are cool, bright and clear. We cover this in more detail when we look at creating a colour palette.

87

At this stage you simply need to be clear on which season you're taking your colours from and which season, if any, you'll take secondary influences from. You can pull in texture, pattern or fonts from another season with real success, as long as you use your designer's eye to make sure that what you're producing is a well-crafted and balanced design.

One more point: you can have one dominant season and only one subordinate. Any more than that and you'll just come across as confused. Be bold and brave, and refine your brief if needs be.

THE CREATIVE MEETING

By now you will hopefully have a notebook full of ideas as well as a great deal of focus. Now it's time to move on to some creative thinking. We're going to brainstorm some concepts as well as pull together the mood board that will set the tone for your brand identity. By the end of this chapter you will be ready to start designing with all the clarity and vision you need.

Whether you're working through this with colleagues or alone, I'd suggest you spend 10 minutes or so presenting, or reminding yourself of your brief: make it clear what the objectives of the project are, and explain your key brand values. What do you need to communicate, and what look and feel are you hoping for? Define your top three and put them somewhere prominent – on a whiteboard for example, so that everyone is clear from the outset what they are working towards. Agree on which season your business should be (it will be better if they have an understanding of colour psychology before you start the session). And be clear about what this means for your design: for example if you're a winter business that means clear, intense and bright colours with strong patterns.

"CREATIVITY IS CONTAGIOUS. PASS IT ON."

- ALBERT EINSTEIN

CREATING YOUR VISION BOARD

Your vision board, or mood board, is going to help you get focused and act as a springboard for your initial design concepts. You're going to create something that really encapsulates how you'd like your brand to look and feel. It's a visual translation of all that focus work we did in Chapter Two, **Planning**, and it will be highly inspirational. Expect lots of light bulb moments!

YOU WILL NEED

A2 or A3 foamboard or mountboard in a colour that you respond to (keep it fairly neutral).

A stash of magazines and catalogues.

Pantone chips, paint chips or other colour guides.

An assortment of odds and ends: ribbons, buttons, flowers, small ornaments: whatever inspires you!

Patterns from fabric, wallpaper samples, packaging etc.

Washi tape or glue.

Scissors.

Start by reminding yourself of the three words that best sum up how you'd like your brand to look and feel. With those words in mind, gather together images, fonts, colours, patterns and any other texture or items you choose that you respond to at an instinctive level. Don't analyse anything at this point. Just pull out what you're drawn to. You'll probably spend around an hour on this stage.

Have a break to recharge your batteries and give yourself a bit of space to work through your pile. Analyse each image or cutting and ask yourself what you feel it says about your brand. What story does it tell? If it tells a strong story, it stays. If it gives you an insight into how you want your brand to look and feel, it stays. If you don't really have a reason for it other than you like it, then get rid of it. Keep going back to your three words and asking yourself, 'Does this support the message I want to communicate?'

You'll probably find that you are able to cull hundreds of images down to an A2 or A3 mood board. It's exciting to see how everything comes together and you should find that the process sparks ideas that will enhance your brand. Ideas for things like your tone of voice, little extras that you might use, textures that are inspired from an abstract image. If you think laterally, you'll really enjoy this!

Once you have finalised your selection of images, use your trims, embellishments and ornaments, where appropriate, to create a mood board that really encapsulates what you're trying to achieve with your branding. Use your washi tape or glue to stick everything down onto your board and there you have it, one inspirational mood board!

From your board you should have an idea of the sorts of fonts, colours, patterns and textures that you'd like to incorporate into your new brand identity and we'll cover how to go about selecting each of these as you work through the rest of the process.

It's the thought process you go through that will make all the difference in creating a brand that's authentically you. So relish the creative process in this chapter and you'll find it pays off long term.

Naturally this mood board isn't going to fit in your notebook, but it's incredibly inspiring to just have around. Perhaps prop it up by your desk or in your office somewhere, to keep you reminded of the big vision you've set yourself, and keep your design on track.

If you're not designing your brand identity yourself, you will still find this process helpful in clarifying your thoughts and understanding which designer is right for you. Use your mood board as a guide when you view each portfolio and ask yourself: 'Does what I see on this website reflect what I'm hoping to achieve with my mood board?'

92

CREATING A ROUTE FORWARDS

If you're rebranding an existing business rather than styling a brand for a new venture, you might find that with a few tweaks, you can salvage some of what you're currently using, whilst creating a completely new look and feel.

When I was running my brand styling agency, many clients would tell me that they needed a new logo. What they actually meant was that they wanted to shake up how their company looked and felt. More often than not it wasn't the logo that needed changing at all, but everything around it.

When you change the fonts, colours, shapes, patterns, textures, illustrations and photography on, say, a website, you can create a wholly different look and feel: one that has the effect you're looking for. And as you'll see as you work through this book, your logo is a very small part of your brand identity.

Be mindful before you throw everything out and think about whether you are able to retain any of your current brand identity. Perhaps you'd like to change the font of your company name but retain the icon? Maybe the icon needs redrawing but the logotype is fine? Perhaps it's just a case of updating the colours? Maybe you really do need to throw everything out and start again. What matters is that you really stand back and make a conscious decision about what needs to happen.

ASSESS WHAT YOU HAVE

Gather together everything you use to promote your business: from your business cards and letterhead to your invoices, leaflets, brochures and packaging. Take screenshots of your website and blog, print them out and collect any adverts that you currently use. If your staff wear a uniform or you have a shopfront or van, take pictures of those and add them to your collection. Lay your marketing collateral out across a big table and ask yourself what you see.

What impression does what you're currently using send out? How consistent is your current brand identity? What messages are your choice of fonts and colours giving? How does your photography represent your business?

If you were to put together a brand board of your current brand identity (see p174 for details on how to do exactly that) how would it look? In fact, if you have the time why not have a go? It's a great way of objectively viewing what you have right now.

Ask yourself: 'What changes do I need to make to ensure my brand identity supports my business vision?' And it's not just about looks; get the feel of your business right and you'll find that your brand identity is an asset, attracting the right sort of attention, creating desire and galvanising action.

Every element you choose, from the font you use on your blog to the colour of your envelopes matters. They all add up to an overall feel. Give yours a consciously put-together look that has the effect you want.

Glue everything into your journal or scrapbook along with the answers to your questions above. Are you starting to feel a little more in control? Like this branding thing might actually get nailed this time? I do hope so!

DIY OR OUTSOURCE?

This is probably a good time to check in and start thinking about whether you're up for styling your own brand or whether you should work with a designer. There are many valid reasons to go down either route. A great brand stylist can be worth their weight in gold, freeing you up to do what you do best, seeing what you may not, and creating the most inspirational and compelling face for your business.

On the flipside, perhaps you are confident that you are best placed to style your brand. Maybe you want complete creative control or perhaps you simply can't afford to invest in design right now. Whatever your reasons, let's just be sure that you're going down the right route.

FINDING THE RIGHT APPROACH FOR YOU

By now it's likely that you'll be bursting with excitement, your head filling up with creative ideas. You will be looking forward to dusting down your design skills and creating something truly exceptional.

The alternative, of course, is that now you see what's involved, you're starting to feel slightly queasy at the enormity of what you're about to tackle. This is your business. It matters that you get this right and you're worried that you just don't have the skills.

That's ok too. You might find that once you have read the guidance on colour and typography it all starts to fall into place and isn't nearly as scary as you first thought. But there's a lot to be said for sticking to what you do best. This book is about helping you understand the process and making better choices.

STYLING YOUR OWN BRAND

Assuming you're up for the job, let's just explore for a moment whether you have the capability and capacity to Do It Yourself. Styling your own brand can be fun, creative and immensely rewarding.

It is also time consuming, requires a certain amount of expertise and can be frustrating at times. Being so close to your business can make it difficult to be objective and it can be easy to lose focus unless you are very disciplined. Follow my advice about writing down a concise brief and you will avoid much of this.

Ask yourself whether you really have the time and skills or whether your time would be better spent driving your business forwards whilst you work with a designer who can stretch and challenge your vision for your business.

Only you can decide whether you are up to the challenge, and certainly by the time we reach the end of this book together, you will know whether it's something you would like to take on or not.

Whichever route you choose, remember, this should be a fun, inspirational and creative project.

Overleaf you'll find invaluable guidance on how to choose the right graphic designer and plenty more throughout the book on how to maintain a positive working relationship, evaluate the work that's produced and facilitate a powerful brand identity.

THE DEFINITIVE GUIDE TO CHOOSING THE RIGHT DESIGNER

Working with the right designer is inspirational, reassuring and utterly thrilling. A great designer will enable you to see your business in a new and exciting light. They will listen to you, yet not be constrained by your ideas. And they will have the skill and creativity to create a vision that surpasses all your expectations.

Over time you might find that your designer or agency becomes a core part of your team, as excited about your successes as you are.

Outsourcing your branding project will allow you to continue to drive your business forwards whilst at the same time being able to stand back and manage the design process objectively and productively. But finding the right designer is a little more challenging than simply running a quick internet search and firing off two or three quote requests.

It's also going to take more than a plea for recommendations from your tried and trusted network, although they can be a good starting point, or working with a friend of a friend.

If you're serious about getting this right, you must take the trouble to pick the right person to style your brand. Working with a designer who doesn't specialise in brand identity can mean a lot of heartache, frustration and wasted time and money. Select your brand stylist for the right reasons and you'll ensure that your journey is a positive one.

FINDING A BRAND STYLIST

From web developers to web designers, marketeers to brand strategists, graphic designers to brand designers and brand stylists, there are many people that *could* help you style your brand. Each will probably come with a different price tag and almost certainly a different skill set, but some of them will be better placed to help your business with other projects.

One of the first clues as to whether you have found the right potential partner is from their website. You are looking for a brand stylist, a graphic designer or a brand identity designer.

You're not really looking for a web designer – they are better placed to help you once you have your brand beautifully styled, and you're certainly not looking for a web developer or IT person. They are technically focused and are highly unlikely to have the skills, experience or creative flair for this particular project.

The most important thing is that you find someone who can deliver the design style you're looking for.

Go back to your inspiration boards on Pinterest, your mood board and your notebooks. Who designed the projects you love? Take some time to browse through their websites, looking closely at their portfolio and process and ask yourself the questions opposite.

I'd recommend you shortlist five or six prospective designers based on their websites. You can be shallow here – brand styling is about looks, so you should expect these people to have gorgeous websites.

Bear in mind that the wonders of technology mean that you don't need to work with someone within fifteen miles of your office. So don't be afraid to approach that fabulous company on another continent. It could be the best decision you ever make.

SHORTLISTING

The portfolio and design style questions are really important here. And they matter whether you are working with a friend of a friend or a well-respected agency. Every designer or agency has their own style and the responsibility lies with you to ensure you pick the right person for the job.

Choose someone whose work inspires you and you've just made everything that happens further down the line fifteen times easier. If you

FIVE QUESTIONS TO ASK YOURSELF
ABOUT A PROSPECTIVE DESIGNER

1 **Does their style reflect what I'm looking for?** This is more important than someone that specialises in your industry – you need to be able to *see* that they can execute what you want.

2 **Do I like their portfolio?** This is obvious but essential. You would be amazed at how many people pick a designer because of their personality rather than their portfolio. You don't have to like everything in there, but you should find two or three standout pieces that you really love.

3 **Do I like what they are saying?** Do I want to work with these people? Do I like their approach? Do I trust them to do a good job?

4 **Is their portfolio cohesive?** Can you see a style? Do they work in a particular industry that's relevant to your business?

5 **Do I like their website?** Is it up to date? It should be! This is what these people do for a living. Do you like the way they've styled their own brand?

select someone based on price alone, the fact that they're prepared to barter with you, or out of loyalty, then you may find that the process that follows is like wading through treacle. You need to be hardheaded here. This is your business, it's your living on the line, you owe it to yourself to work with the right person.

Once you've shortlisted your agencies or designers, I recommend you send a quick email outlining your project and see what comes back.

At the risk of stating the obvious, notice how quickly they respond, whether they send you anything in the mail, and how interested they seem in your project. Do they give you the impression that they want your business? Do you get the feeling they will be responsive to work with or are they slow even at the pre-sales stage? Do they send you anything that excites you? Are you looking forward to meeting these people? Trust your gut as well as your head.

You are best placed to decide how many you shortlist to meet, either online or in person, but two or three is probably a good number.

WEIGHING UP YOUR OPTIONS

Make notes in your journal after every meeting as it's so easy to be overwhelmed at this point. Obviously money comes into it, of course it does, but it's important to get this right and you can't make this sort of decision based on price alone.

As well as what the agency or designer costs, consider what you will get within that price as every designer will have a different process and pricing strategy. Are they offering a fixed project fee (within reason?) or are you dealing with an open-ended bill? Are they quoting you for just a logo or the whole shebang?

What sorts of questions did they ask you? Did they want to know about the sort of impression you were looking for or uncreative basics like the

SHORTLISTING

AFTER YOUR MEETING

Is this company excited about my project? Do they seem inspired by what I'm trying to achieve?

Do they want my business? The right agency or freelance designer will want your business, not just for the money but the creative potential too.

Do I feel they would do a good job? What sorts of questions do they ask you? Do they challenge you? Do they get you to think beyond your comfort zone? And how does that feel?

Am I inspired by what they could do? Get them to tell you the story behind the pieces in the portfolio that you like. What was the reason that they used specific colours/ fonts/ devices in those designs? Do you like their approach?

What direction will they take your brand identity in? Whilst it's unlikely they will tell you precisely, how they will style your brand (this sort of creative process takes time), they will probably have a good idea of the sort of direction they'd like to take your brand identity in. Do they 'get' your brief?

Do I want to work with them? How do you feel at the end of the meeting? Did you get on well? Was there a good chemistry and mutual trust?

How much do they cost and what will I get for my money? Look closely at what you're getting from each designer and whether there's anything you can leave out if needs be. It would be such a shame to miss out on working with your dream team because of price, so make sure you're comparing on an equal playing field.

How many concepts do they deliver? This is one example of where more definitely doesn't mean better value. Two or three concepts will give you the benefit of your designers' focus whilst also giving you a focused answer to a very specific brief.

What happens if I don't like the designs? Be clear from the outset what you're getting for your money. Some designers will give you a project fee, others will charge you more if they need to rework a design. This doesn't need to be a bad thing but you do need to know where you stand upfront.

colours you like and the sorts of fonts you want to see. If you're looking for someone to deliver above and beyond your imagination, they need to be talking to you about your business aspirations rather than the mechanics of what you're looking for.

What sorts of projects will they be able to help you with once your brand identity has been styled? This certainly shouldn't be a deal breaker, but it's helpful to know what they can help you with further down the line so that you can make an informed decision.

And whilst I know it's tempting to go with the company who can do the whole lot – from initial concept through to the build of a very technical website, there is a lot to be said for working with real specialists, especially if you're on a tight budget.

You're much better off working with an exceptionally talented creative and then moving on to a super smart web developer rather than trying to work with one person who promises to be able to do the lot. I am yet to meet a creative genius who also has a head for serious coding and would always rather work with two separate specialists than one jack of all trades.

If you put this level of thought into choosing your designer you should find that the process is an enjoyable, empowering and self-affirming one. You'll be inspired, invigorated and energised and the effect on your business will be palpable. High five anyone?

GETTING OFF TO THE RIGHT START

Working with a designer should be a positive experience and you both have a role to play in ensuring that your project runs smoothly. Here are some tips to help you get your project off to the very best possible start.

Own your decision By following the steps above, you've taken yourself through a robust process and you should know, in your heart and your head, that you've made the right decision. Make peace with your choice, resist the temptation to let buyer's remorse undermine your confidence in your decision. Trust your designer!

Ask for deadlines Agreeing a timetable for the scope of works is an essential part of a good working relationship. If your designer isn't forthcoming with project milestones, ask if you can agree when you'll see a first draft and how much time revisions will take after that. Setting these dates is very reassuring and is something any professional will be glad to do.

Trust your designer Once you've briefed your designer resist the temptation to get in touch every few days to 'manage the process' or check on progress. Trust that your designer has enough information to create something fabulous for you and leave them to get on with their job.

Don't confuse things Part of the skill in being a good brand stylist lies in creating clarity from a complex brief, so don't muddy the waters by sending through daily updates with information that you'd forgotten about, unless it's absolutely game-changing to the design process. Your designer doesn't need the minutiae of your plans, they just need the headlines.

CHAPTER FOUR

CREATE YOUR LOGO

"BE YOURSELF.
EVERYONE ELSE IS TAKEN."
- OSCAR WILDE

Your logo is the one device that will allow current and potential customers to recognise your business in an instant; it should be strong, unique and confident. A well-designed logo will enable you to stand out from the crowd and communicate confidence and professionalism.

And whilst fonts, textures, patterns and photography enable you to create a really strong emotive connection with your customers and build personality, a powerful logo will set the tone for your business. Your logo is the cornerstone of your brand identity.

Your logo should be timeless. Resist the temptation to create anything too 'off-the-wall' that you might come to regret later. You can mix up your brand assets every few years, allowing your brand identity to evolve as trends come and go, but your logo will be with you for a long time.

Of all the elements in your brand identity you might create yourself, this is probably the one to outsource if you're feeling remotely under-confident about your design skills.

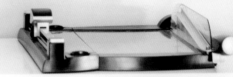

THE ANATOMY OF A DISTINCTIVE LOGO

Your logo may include some, or all, of the elements below.

THE DEVICE OR ICON

This is what many of us think of as a 'logo'. It's the picture that might communicate what you do in a very literal way, or perhaps it communicates something about your business in a more abstract way.

THE LOGOTYPE

This is the font your company name is written in. It might be a simple font, it may have a distinctive twist or have been modified in some way to create something unique to you. It should be legible and communicate the right tone.

THE STRAPLINE

This is most often used to describe what your business does if the name doesn't make it clear, or to communicate what makes your business unique. It almost always appears with your logo but it doesn't have to.

A STRONG STATEMENT *Above.*
Boutique catering company Whoa Nelly's logo design is both clean and distinctive. Caava Design balanced this contemporary logo with an equally modern typeface collection and beautiful botanical fruit illustrations to create a memorable and impactful identity. See page 195 for more.

LOGO STYLES

There are numerous ways to execute a logo and the route you take is likely to vary depending on your business and your brief. Some company names lend themselves to a visual logo more than others. It's very easy to create an illustration for a chair designer or a horse whisperer for example. It's much harder to draw what a management consultant does. You may also find that your overall brief dictates what's appropriate: an expressive logo might lend itself to a distinctive, signature style logo, whilst a more contemporary brief might lend itself to a more minimalist logotype. Let the brief guide you in your approach.

If you're concerned about your illustrative skills, or are struggling to come up with an innovative concept for your device, then I highly recommend you focus on creating a simple logotype.

With the right typeface and colour combination, careful spacing and simple layout, you can create something distinctive and classy. A logo that is simple and well executed is always going to make a bigger impact than something that has a great concept behind it, but is a little rough around the edges.

LOGOTYPE

Logotypes put a distinctive typeface at the heart of the logo, sometimes incorporating a clever twist to create something unique and striking. You might incorporate an icon into a letter, replace a letter with a shape, or add an embellishment to the word to create something distinctive. Logotypes are strong, simple and confident.

LITERAL

Can you draw what your business does? Does your company name or business activity lend itself to something visual? Literal logos can add visual depth to your brand identity as well as creating meaning and interest.

LATERAL

Lateral logos can make a bold statement. Is there a story behind your brand that could lend itself to something visual? Can you generate any ideas from your brand values or the way you like to work?

GIVE YOUR LOGO THE PROFESSIONAL TREATMENT

Your logo is usually the first and last thing a client will see. From an initial piece of promotional literature or advert, to your invoice or receipt at the end of a transaction, your logo is a constant, and highly prominent, representation of your business.

The best logos are simple, distinctive and exquisitely designed. Sometimes they're clever, sometimes they're quirky and sometimes they are unusual. What matters most of all is that they look professional. Here's how:

BALANCE AND PROPORTION

Balance is at the heart of good design, never more so than in a logo. Balance between the logotype and strapline, balance between the icon and logotype if you have one, and balance between the typefaces and colours. Use the 'rule of thirds' to create something that feels well proportioned and assured.

SIMPLICITY

Resist the temptation to create an elaborate illustration that encapsulates everything your business does along with your company history. Simple and iconic is often best.

STYLE

Your logo should be aspirational, strong and confident, whatever your brand style. This means paying serious attention to the fine details and ensuring that the end result is nothing less than exquisite.

TYPE

Many of the most stylish logos don't have an icon at all, they use a strong font to convey a feeling and make a strong mark. Whether you're using an icon or not, make sure your logo stands out from the crowd with a remarkable typeface. Or put a twist on the font to create something unique.

CHARACTER, STYLE AND PERSONALITY

Each of the logos on this page sends out a very strong and confident message. Some are soft and whimsical, others clean and contemporary. What they all have in common is self assurance in their style. And that in itself is very compelling.

UNIQUE

The best logos convey a feeling about a business, they communicate what a company does and they often put a clever spin on a simple concept. A simple typeface with a clever twist; an illustration that makes you look twice, or an engaging, hand-lettered logotype will set you apart from the crowd. Avoid Clipart and standard issue fonts like the plague.

INTELLIGENT

The 'picture' isn't what makes the logo. It's enough to have a powerful typeface that should liberate you. Avoid clichés. A stylish font that is well spaced and demonstrates the right character about, for instance, a chiropractic clinic, is going to be far more successful than a mere picture of a human spine above your logo. You don't necessarily need a device to get value for money out of your logo design.

COLOUR

Colour increases recognition and enables you to create an emotive connection with your client. The right colours will look attractive together, engage and attract your most profitable clients, and subconsciously communicate your brand values.

APPEALING

A logo should be something nice to look at. You should be proud of how it represents your business. Invest time in creating something truly distinctive and unique.

SCALEABLE

From a business card or a small item of packaging through to a shopfront or side of a truck, your logo should work at multiple sizes. This comes down partly to technical considerations in the way your logo is created (more on this later) but also practically, does it work when you scale it, or does it lose impact?

114

ROMY COLLÉ

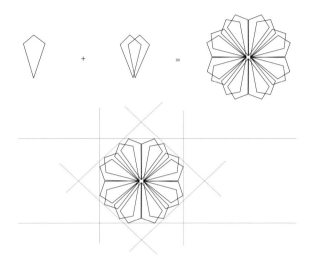

INSPIRED BY NATURE This intricate logo design by Revival Designbüro for jewellery designer Romy Collé was inspired by the wings on a favourite brooch. When brought together en masse, the result is strikingly elegant and perfectly positions the brand at the premium end of the market.

EVALUATING YOUR CURRENT LOGO

If you have a logo at the moment, ask yourself how your current logo measures up to the guidelines on pages 112-114. Consider the message that the typeface, colours and device are communicating. Which of them has the impact you're looking for? Are you happy with each element? Do you need to refine any or all of the parts?

Is your logo fit for purpose? Does it support your brand message? Is it simple, stylish and strong? Does it give your business the confidence and professionalism you deserve? Is it going to get you where you want to be?

You may find that you need to scrap what you have and start again. Or maybe you could tweak it and emerge with something that you're proud of.

DESIGNING A DISTINCTIVE LOGO

Whether you're planning on designing your own logo or working with a graphic designer, having an understanding of the process will make sure it stays fun and gives you the very best result for your unique business.

BRAINSTORMING CONCEPTS

Starting your logo design journey with a healthy dose of research means that you'll be buoyed up with inspiration before you put pen to paper. Seek out logos that inspire you, from those in your industry to companies that you simply admire. Ask yourself 'Why do I like this?' and 'How would I make this my own?' Take inspiration from as many sources as possible but be sure that the ideas you come up with are all your own.

Challenge yourself to sketch out as many ideas as possible within twenty minutes. Don't analyse at this point, simply let your mind wander and the ideas flow. Think literally and laterally. Explore clever ideas with logotypes as well as more literal and abstract ideas.

As you assess each idea ask yourself 'Does this support my brand message?' 'Does this fit in with what we are trying to achieve?' and 'Would I be proud to have this represent my company?'.

Take forward only your strongest ideas, try mocking them up and seeing how they work. And if you find that none of them are up to scratch, that's fine. Take a break, come back to it another day and run another creative brainstorming session. You will crack this!

PRETTY DETAILED This delicate logo design for British florist, Bare Blooms, is both thoughtful and beautiful. Look at the detail in the illustrated B device, isn't it just lovely?

BareBlooms

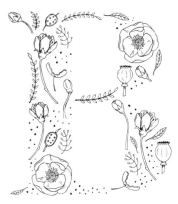

Aline Bouma

CREATING YOUR LOGO

118

Once you have a concept you're happy with, you're ready to translate it into something real.

You will need a pen, pencil and paper for any sketching or illustrations you do; a camera or scanner to capture your illustrations and transfer them to your computer; a Mac or PC and a graphics package.

It's best to create your logo in a vector design package like Adobe Illustrator. These programmes are designed for this very purpose and you'll find them packed with functionality that will help you tweak and refine your logo.

If you're new to working with these programmes, it will be worth taking some online training seminars. There are plenty of free tutorials and a couple of hours spent here can go a long way.

You *could* create a logo in PowerPoint or even Microsoft Word, but to be honest, these programmes were never designed for this purpose and you are going to find it very difficult to place each graphic element precisely, not to mention manipulating your type with precision.

Assuming that you have a suitable graphics package in place, let's think about the steps. Depending on the design approach you've taken, and your concept, the steps required might be very different; but broadly speaking you need to create a logotype, add your device if appropriate, colour your logo and then create a scaleable and useable file across multiple platforms.

COLOUR PSYCHOLOGY CONSIDERATIONS

Your logo style will be led, as with all of your brand elements, by your seasonal personality.

A winter logo is likely to be strong, dramatic and clean. Perhaps it will use geometric shapes and clear, bright, intense colours? A spring logo will feel approachable, warm and clear with fine lines and perhaps use circles. It will use light, bright and clear colours.

A summer logo will be refined, elegant and have a feel of quality about it. Colours are likely to be cool, delicate and muted. An autumn logo will have a robust, substantial, perhaps organic feel to it. Colours will be warm, intense and muted, fonts will have an element of substance to them and shapes will be strong with rounded corners.

Take a look at the logos on page 113 and see if you can work out what season they are!

Whatever season your business is, your logo should support your brand values, and colour psychology is a reliable way of doing that.

CRAFTING YOUR LOGOTYPE

Since you're going to build your logo around your company name, it makes sense to start with your logotype.

Starting with a clean document in your design programme, simply type your company name into a new text box. You may wish to use multiple text boxes if you plan to be creative with the layout, perhaps just one depending on your concept. Play around with various elements until you have something you're happy with.

It's a good idea to duplicate your design once you've created something you like, so you can continue to experiment whilst modifying small details. Fine tuning will make all the difference to the professionalism of your final logo, so don't underestimate the importance of getting the detail right.

THE TYPEFACE

Do you have a font in mind that you'd like to use? I recommend that you invest in something well designed and distinctive from a professional font foundry rather than using one of the fonts that came with your computer. We're working hard here to create a stylish and unique brand identity and that means borrowing some tricks from professional graphic designers. And just as you wouldn't catch a pro using a system font, so you shouldn't either.

Fonts aren't usually expensive, anything from £3 to £60 ($5 to $100) is around average, and when you think of the money you're saving by styling your own brand, it's worth a little investment to achieve the strength and individuality your business warrants. See the resources section on page 203 for a list of my favourite places to buy fonts.

FROM CONCEPT TO COMPLETION *Opposite* Brand Stylist Angela Scheffer sketched multiple concepts for this luxurious brand identity for Kate Whelan Events before digitising her ideas to present to the client. Following feedback and input from Kate, the final brand board includes sub marks, pattern and fonts to add impact and personality.

3

COLORS

BRONZE | BLACK | TAUPE | CREAM

SUB MARK   SECONDARY LOGO

KATE WHELAN
events

TAGLINE

events
OF EXTRAORDINARY DETAIL

FONTS

GOTHAM EX   NEVIS BOLD

ABCDEFGHIJKLMNOPQRSTUVWXYZ

PATTERNS

The font you use for your logo should be distinctive and once you've used it in the logo, you shouldn't really use it elsewhere, so pick carefully. Using the same font for your logo and then, say, your website headings, will weaken your logo so keep the two very distinct. I like to shortlist a dozen or so fonts and play around with a few before making my final selection.

You need to consider how the font for your logo works in conjunction with your other brand elements so you may find that you need to tweak and refine your initial ideas as you work through the process.

DESIGN YOUR LOGO LIKE A PRO

LETTER SPACING

Play about with the letter spacing, perhaps increasing or decreasing until you find the right balance. As a general rule, increasing the spacing will make your logo feel more light, airy and upmarket. Decreasing the space between the letters will add more drama and impact, especially when combined with a condensed, uppercase font. Experiment with different styles until you find one that works for you.

HIERARCHY

If you have a long company name with multiple words, ask yourself whether each word needs equal emphasis. Words such as 'the' or 'company' might work better in a smaller font above or below the main word(s).

If you play with scale, do just make sure that your sizes are balanced, using the 'rule of thirds' to ensure the proportions feel right.

i heart
ORGANIZING
FAMILY · HOME · LIFE

i heart
ORGANIZING
FAMILY · HOME · LIFE

BRIGHT AND BOLD
This makeover for I Heart Organizing mixes clear, intense colours with plenty of white space for an uncluttered and inspirational vibe.

i heart
ORGANIZING
family . home . life

i Heart
ORGANIZING
FAMILY · HOME · LIFE

i heart
ORGANIZING
family . home . life

CASE

Should your name be written uppercase or lowercase? Uppercase adds gravitas and authority whilst lowercase feels more approachable and informal. Which is right for your business? Generally title case never looks great, so stick with one or the other.

CONTRAST

Most fonts come in various weights and it can be good to experiment to see which works best for your logo. Contrast is good. So pairing a bold or black typeface with a light font can be effective. Avoid using similar weights, such as regular and bold or bold and black where possible.

PERSONALISATION

Converting your font to 'outlines' or 'curves' will change its properties, changing it from editable type to an image that you can manipulate. Once you're broadly happy with the layout of your logotype, experiment with changing the details and creating something that's your own. This is by no means an essential step and is best suited to advanced users of Adobe Illustrator. There are plenty of tutorials online if you'd like to have a go.

YOUR ICON OR DEVICE

One of the most effective ways to create a unique icon is to hand draw something yourself. Then either scan or photograph it to transfer it to your computer. Next, use a programme like Illustrator to trace the image. To do this you simply place your image in a new document and go to Object> Image > Expand and Make. You can then colourise and refine your icon until you have something that works for you.

DESIGNING YOUR STRAPLINE

Your strapline, or business descriptor, is something that usually sits underneath your logo and provides either more information on what your business does or positions you clearly in the market.

Your strapline will be best if it's concise. You can also consider creating multiple straplines for different situations if you need to.

Use the font of your strapline to add a different dimension and personality to your logo. You can play about with combinations that will give the right balance and edge to your design, which in turn will introduce different facets of your business values.

Do remember that your logo will be shrunk down to fit on a business card, and your strapline should be legible at that size too. Experiment with fonts, sizing and letter spacing until you have something you're happy with.

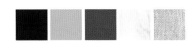

SETTING OUT YOUR LOGO

Once you have your distinct elements, it's time to pull them together and see how they work.

There are a number of basic ways of setting out your logo and playing about with the various options will help you decide which works best for you. Remember that you can also add in lines, shapes or boxes at this point to give the whole thing a cohesive and unique feel. As always, take your lead from what inspires you and what feels right for your business, but most of all ask yourself: 'How can I make this my own?'

GIVE YOURSELF OPTIONS There are so many ways to lay out a logo, as these concepts for a design and build firm demonstrate. Experiment with layouts until you find something that feels right.

As you experiment with layouts, consider how you might be using your logo moving forwards. Where do you need to use it? If you have a very particular size of packaging on which the logo will need to work, does the logo lend itself to being especially tall, wide or square, for example?

Your final logo will need to be saved as a single item within a file. Remember that design is rarely a linear process, so you may find that once you view your logo as a part of the rest of your brand identity, you need to make further refinements until you're completely happy with everything.

PRACTICALITIES

Your logo will need to be used both very small and potentially very large, so it's important it works at every size. Here are a few sense checks many professionals use to be sure that what they are creating will work.

1 Is it clear from the combination of logo, strapline, company name and device what your business does?

2 Can the logo be scaled to any size without losing clarity? Is the quality sufficient that the edges look crisp and clean even when blown up? Scale-up your logo so that it fills a page. Print out and just check that everything looks as smart and professional as you'd like it to. You can easily rectify anything that's a bit rough around the edges now. It's much harder to do once the vinyl for your new shopfront has been cut and mounted.

3 Create a business-card sized box, 85 x 55mm (3.5 x 2in), and paste your logo inside, leaving at least 5mm (1/4in) space from each edge. Is the strapline legible when scaled down? As a general rule your strapline should be a minimum of 6pt when used at this size.

Does your icon work and is your logotype legible at this size? If not, how can you adapt it to work?

Print out the business card mockup and take a look at the print-out. It's amazing what you can spot when you have something on paper in front of you.

4 Whether your logo will work in black and white is not so relevant as it might have been 20 years ago, when photocopiers and fax machines could not reproduce in colour, but you might wish to have your logo printed in a single colour for certain instances. Would this work without losing your message?

SAVING YOUR LOGO FOR USE

ACROSS MULTIPLE PLATFORMS

Whatever your business, it's likely that you will need:

A vector EPS file for print work Convert all your text to outlines and export as an EPS file. You'll be able to scale this to any size.

A JPEG for use online You'll need to open your file in a photo editing package like Adobe Photoshop and Save for Web to produce a highly optimised file.

A GIF or PNG file which will produce a very small file size of high quality if your logo only uses a couple of colours

You may also wish to think about creating **a 'favicon'** of your icon or device. At 90 x 90 pixels, this favicon sits in the top left of your browser's address bar.

CHAPTER FIVE

PULLING TOGETHER YOUR BRAND ELEMENTS

"BE A VOICE, NOT AN ECHO."

- ALBERT EINSTEIN

130

Pattern, texture, colour and illustrative devices are the elements that bring personality and style to your brand identity. They are the bits that create the emotive connection and enable you to create a brand that really resonates with your current and prospective clients.

And whether you already have a logo design that you love, or you're working through this process from start to finish, you'll find that it's in this section that your brand styling really starts to take shape. This is the accessorising of your brand that will make all the difference to not only how your brand looks, but most importantly, how it **feels**.

PACKING A PUNCH These gorgeous patterns for Jill Smith have been turned into bespoke wrapping paper that take her brand communications to a whole new level. See the rest of Jill's brand identity on p26.

"YOU WILL NEVER INFLUENCE THE WORLD BY TRYING TO BE LIKE IT."

YOUR BRAND COLOURS

Colour has the power to make us feel. Happy, inspired, uplifted or creative; calm, collected, relaxed and in control; passionate, fired-up, confident and energised; successful, decisive, perceptive and discerning. Colour can evoke all of these emotions subconsciously within us.

And whilst colour may be a very personal, emotive choice, the rules of colour psychology will help you make smarter, more objective choices to help your business communicate in the way you would like it to.

In this section you're going to put together a colour palette based on both your brand values that we teased out in Chapter Two, **Planning** and your seasonal colour personality in Chapter Three, **Create Your Vision**. Let's start by focusing on which colours will best support your business message.

FINDING THE COLOURS TO SUPPORT YOUR BRAND VALUES

It's time to refer to the list of core business values and the notes you made in the Planning chapter. Ask yourself: 'How do I want my potential clients to see my business?'; 'What do I need people to know?' and 'What words would I use to describe how I'd like my business to come across? You'll probably have a shortlist of around eight or ten words.

Each colour will support a different value. Let's start by identifying which colours your business needs to use in order to communicate your core messages. We'll then move on to selecting a colour palette that authentically reflects you and your brand.

When you pull together colours from the same season, you'll create a harmonious colour palette that communicates the positive elements of each colour and season. If you inadvertently mix colours from across the seasons: say a muted (summer) green with a strong, intense (winter) blue you'll create discord and that's when the negative elements of the season and colour will come to the fore.

Remember that every colour (with the exception of black) will appear in every season. Be led by the colours that work for your brand and choose tones that fit within your season. We'll look at pulling together a colour palette and selecting your shades once you've identified which colours are right for your business. Let's start by taking a look at a range of colours and their attributes.

MODERN MEXICAN This colourful brand identity for drinks company Chinampas was inspired by the traditional colours and patterns of Mexican arts, crafts and culture. Given a very modern and striking twist by UK branding agency Tonik, the pattern can be employed across a wide range of stationery and packaging for maximum impact.

THE MEANING OF COLOUR

PURPLE

Visionary, purposeful, truthful, authentic, luxurious, content, spiritual, quality. Flaky, mystical, downmarket.

Purple is a great go-to colour for businesses on a mission. A deep purple will exude strength and vision, whilst also feeling approachable. It makes a great alternative to black if your business isn't winter. A softer, lighter purple will feel much calmer, serene and relaxing, whilst a light violet has a spiritual quality about it.

BLUE

Intelligent, logical, ordered, calm, efficient, cool, serene, trustworthy, soothing, clear, forward thinking, communicative, focused, reflective. Cold, unfriendly, unemotional, conservative.

Blue is a very popular colour and brings with it a wide gamut of attributes. But which blue to choose? A deep, petrol blue balances blue with a little green and a hint of black and so will feel intelligent, strong and highly trustworthy. It's the ideal tone for communicating planning, logic and order. A bright, intense cyan will be, by contrast, more about clarity and communication whilst a soft, light blue will feel reflective, calm and serene.

TURQUOISE

Inspirational, innovative, creative, fresh ideas, efficient, clarity of thought, compassionate, calming, healing, self-sufficient. Aloof, demanding, unreliable, boastful.

From the richest teal exuding strength, efficiency and integrity to the softest, prettiest aquas, turquoise brings a diverse character depending on its tone.

A mix of blue, green and yellow, Turquoise combines many of their attributes. The calm, communicative qualities of blue blend with the growth and balance of green, while the hint of yellow provides an uplift that we associate so well with this colour.

134

GREEN

Restful, restorative, balanced, harmonious, abundant. Staid, stagnant, boring.

Green is a restful, balanced and restorative colour that communicates harmony between mind, body and emotions. Green has an instinctive, primal quality about it that relates to an abundance of food and lush growth. It can add a lovely balance and freshness to a colour palette. A deep olive green can add an element of restrained balance and harmony to a summer palette, whilst a bottle green or British racing green has a large element of blue in its make-up and so will communicate more of the logical, efficient and professional attributes you might associate with blue.

YELLOW

Self-confident, high self-esteem, optimistic, happy, friendly, extrovert, emotional strength. Anxious, lacking in confidence, needy.

Yellow is a gloriously happy, optimistic colour, brimming with self-confidence and full of promise. A delicate, primrose yellow will bring a soft and supportive optimism to a spring palette, whilst a warm, intense mustard makes a bold and confident statement.

Yellow can be a difficult colour to work into your brand identity as the paler shades are barely legible when used on a font: certainly only use it on a logo with care. Consider incorporating yellow into patterns or icons if you have a set of brand values that would benefit from this colour.

ORANGE

Creative, abundant, sociable, positive, passionate, sensuous, secure, comfort, energetic. Unsafe, frivolous, deprived.

Orange has certainly suffered from its association with the no-frills sector in recent years, but it's a wonderful colour that deserves consideration for your colour palette. Hues range from the brightest tangerine through feminine corals to soft peaches and apricots. Oranges that have more of a pink tone will add a female tone to your palette, whilst the stronger, redder tones will also take on more the red attributes: strength, stamina and determination.

RED

Strong, assertive, determined, motivated, courageous, warm, energetic, self-starter. Aggressive, demanding, defiant, strain, anger.

Red will make the maximum visual impact for your business and is a great colour if you're in an industry where you need to assert yourself.

Bright, tomato reds make a bold impact in a winter colour palette, whilst a soft, light cherry red will add warmth, energy and strength to a palette of spring pastels that may have otherwise been lacking in oomph. A warm burgundy will add an element of tradition and history.

PINK

Compassionate, warm, nurturing, tranquil, soothing, romantic, intimate, kind, reassuring, intuitive, hopeful, optimistic. Naïve, vulnerable, needy, over-cautious, girlish, lacking of willpower, lack of self worth.

Pink is an unashamedly feminine colour. Soft, blush pinks and nudes add a touch of class and elegance to a pared back palette whilst a bold magenta or neon pink will be altogether more confident.

BROWN

Grounded, stable, reliable, balanced, aspirational, reassured, practical, honest, sincere, warm, industrious, sensual, wholesome, orderly, organised, confident, modest, understated, earthy. Boring, staid, heavy, unsophisticated, stingy, materialistic.

Brown is another great alternative to black and a natural choice for businesses who want to communicate an organic, earthy vibe. When executed with flair, brown can look quietly aspirational and confident. Mix a deep brown with a metallic or a beautiful mint green and you'll create a luxurious and stylish palette. Style that same brown with a bright orange and yellow, and you'll create something altogether more bold.

BLACK

Glamorous, powerful, safe, secure, sophisticated, uncompromising, serious, luxurious, opulent, dramatic, dynamic, substantial, efficient, mysterious and in control. Draining, menacing, oppressive, heavy.

Remember that the misuse of black is the most likely way to throw out your colour palette and communicate some of the negative elements of your colours or seasons. It's a powerful colour for winter businesses and easy to use, but avoid it if your business is spring, summer or autumn.

WHITE

138

Clear, pure, simple efficient, uncompromising, clean, hygienic, illuminating, sophisticated, ethereal. Isolating, uncompromising, stark, standoffish.

You may not add 'white' to your colour palette as such, but it does bring with it a set of characteristics and attributes which are worth considering. Consider how much white you should allow for your finished design. Try giving yourself some 'white space' on your blog or website, or perhaps use some subtle texture or pattern to fill the space.

Polar white, or the stark white found in a minimalist apartment or an art gallery, is as hard to wear or work with as black, and belongs only in the winter palette. For the rest of us think creamy, butter whites, greeny-grey whites or greeny-blue whites. We really are talking about a very subtle amount of colour here. There is a white for every season and visually that's important: it lightens things up and creates freshness.

GOLD

Rich, opulent, warm, successful, wise, enlightened, powerful, successful, wealthy, generous, compassionate, caring, loving, giving. Immature, tacky, unsophisticated, ignorant, fear of success, fear of wealth, mean-spirited, lack of wisdom, selfish, demanding.

SILVER

Reflective, illuminating, prestigious, wealthy, balanced, calming, glamorous, soothing, wise, insightful, self-controlled, responsible, dignified. Lifeless, insincere, non-committal, dull, deceptive, melancholy.

Silver and gold add a luxurious and special touch to your colour palette. They can be expensive to reproduce in print, and on the web will convert to grey or brown, so use as an accent rather than the main colour within your palette.

GREY

Sophisticated, glamorous, substance, efficiency. Oppressive, lacks energy, lifeless, dull, fears exposure.

Grey combines the positive and negative effects of both black and white, and as such can be a useful colour when used with a light hand. Dark charcoals can be invaluable foils for softer, more delicate tones and especially useful when used for body text. They print well and work well online too. Softer, lighter greys can add a touch of sophistication and class to a palette but must be used sparingly or you'll risk sapping the energy out of your design.

HOW TO PUT TOGETHER A COLOUR PALETTE WITH CONFIDENCE

After reading through the colour descriptions on pages 134-139, you are now ready to identify the colours you're looking for. Now comes the fun part: long-listing and short-listing the colours that are going to represent you and your business.

As long as you stick to your core season, you'll find that all the colours will work together, so there is no need to worry about whether everything 'goes'. Pulling colours from the same season means that they will be naturally harmonious and communicate the positive elements of the season and the individual colour.

Ideally you'll need a pantone chip book for this stage, which will enable you to tear out colours you respond to and compare each of them side by side. You'll be able to spot subtle differences in the colours and also pull from a very wide gamut of colours.

Alternatively, use paint chips or colour cards to help you visualise how certain colours might work together and then use the manufacturers' website to colour-pick the make-up. It's not the most sophisticated solution, but it will work if you're determined!

CREATE YOUR LONG LIST

Start by working through the book, tearing out the chips that you respond to. You'll want to ensure that they fit within your season, but we will sort through them later to check that what you put together is cohesive. Right now we are focusing on creating lots of options.

Don't overthink this initial stage, just pull out what you respond to. You'll most likely end up with several of each colour and that's a good thing.

Remember: if your business is spring you'll be looking for light, bright, clear colours that have a softness to them. They'll have an element of white in their make-up and will feel light and inspirational.

If your business is summer, you'll be looking for cool, delicate, muted colours that have a touch of grey in them. Think tasteful Farrow & Ball tones as well as darker blues, greens and reds. navy blue, British racing green and burgundy — they will be deep in tone but will have a coolness about them.

SIX THINGS TO REMEMBER
ABOUT COLOUR

There are no 'right' or 'wrong' colours but some tones will support your brand and others will fight it.

Identify the colours that will support your messaging and then be led by your season to determine the tone and depth of your colours.

Mix colours only from your seasonal personality and you will communicate an authentic message.

Avoid black if your business is not a winter personality.

Be practical. Some lighter colours just won't be legible in fine detail or small fonts: balance your palette with darker tones as well as pales.

Colour is one way to communicate your brand values, type, pattern, illustration and design style will all do this too. Don't overdo your palette if you're more of a restrained person.

141

Autumnal colours are warm, intense and muted. This season has the widest gamut of colours of all and autumn tones have a depth that is discernible even in the lightest shades, where you'll still be looking for a certain warmth and restraint.

A winter colour palette will be made up of bright, clear, strong and intense colours. This is a palette of extremes, the darkest and lightest of tones, each bringing strength and clarity. Now is the time to bring in black, polar white and the deepest of petrol blues. Consider also icy tones to add an air of lightness and stop things getting too heavy.

By all means also go with your heart and your gut as well as your head, especially whilst you're creating your initial long list. You need to love this colour palette, so if you want to add in a turquoise just because you love it, do it! There's no need to over-think things.

CREATE YOUR SHORTLIST

You'll need to do this next step in natural light. So if you're working in the evening or in a dark office, find yourself somewhere to go in daylight and you'll see the colours in their true state.

Lay out your chips and start to look for colours that don't fit. Begin to make choices between which of the subtly different colours are right for your business and which you simply don't like.

Slowly you'll see a palette emerging. Walk away and come back. Does everything fit? Is everything harmonious? By harmonious we mean looking for colours from the same season.

You might be going for a high contrast, energetic palette of bright colours or a quietly confident palette of more low-

contrast, muted shades. What we're looking for is colours to share the same attributes: light, bright and clear for spring and so on. As you do this more and more, you'll start to spot the 'odd one out'. For instance, you'll notice the yellow with slightly too much intensity in amongst the muted, soft and delicate summer colours and you'll swap it for a similar but more harmonious shade.

This is where the chips really come into their own: they enable you to compare and contrast and easily swap in one colour for another. Pantone chip books can be expensive, but it's possible to pick them up sometimes in online auctions for a fraction of the price, and they're certainly a good investment if you plan on styling more than one brand.

CHECK THE PRACTICALITIES

Have you picked out a colour for each of your key brand values? You might find that there are some that just don't work. Perhaps you just can't find a shade that fits with the other colours you've chosen, or perhaps you just don't like one of the shades you need (lots of people have an aversion to orange). That's OK.

Not every single element of your brand personality needs to be communicated through your colour palette. Your typefaces, patterns, logo and even style of design will all complete the picture.

Do you have some darker options that you can use for text? A palette of pretty pastels or soft, muted taupes can be a joy to look at, but will be of little practical use when it comes to colouring text on your website or leaflets. You'll need to balance your softer colours with a good selection of darker tones. Think greys, browns, blues and purples.

TRANSFER YOUR SELECTION TO YOUR DESIGN PROGRAMME

Once you have a colour palette you're happy with, glue the swatches down onto a sheet of paper or straight into your notebook. Don't they look gorgeous?

You'll also need to create a document which contains all of your colours, ready for you to use in your designs. If you're using Adobe InDesign or Illustrator you can simply open a new document and add your colours in the Swatches panel. Delete any colours the programme has already imported and save as a new set of swatches, ready to import into any future design project.

You may also like to create a visual of your colours so that you can see how they will work on screen. You'll

need to do this for your brand book or board so it makes sense to get ahead.

Simply draw a number of shapes, space them evenly and fill with your desired colours. I like to use circles for spring, squares for summer, squares with rounded corners for autumn and octagons for winter, but choose shapes that fit best with your brand.

Hurrah! You now have a colour palette.

USING YOUR COLOURS

As you start to style up your brand and move onto designing specific pieces of literature, remember that everything has a colour.

See beyond the basics of your logo and headings and think also about the colour of your body copy, your social media icons, and the patterns and textures that you choose. Consider the colour of the text on your newsletters, on your blog and even the colour of the hyperlinks on your website. It's this level of attention to detail that will lift your brand styling above the norm.

Embrace your colour palette You've created something that is both considered and powerful. Now that you've pulled together colours with intention, now use them consistently across all your communications for maximum impact.

Black can be so useful, but it's not right for every business. Here are some dark shades that will give you the gravitas and impact you need.

Brown Grounded, earthy, organic. Ideal for an autumnal business, this will also work for a luxury brand when mixed with the right shades.

Deep Blue Logic, efficiency, organisation. A great choice for professional services.

Purple Rich, visionary, authentic. Can feel immensely luxurious, authentic or perhaps even spiritual. An aspirational colour when combined with a metallic.

Bottle Green An earthy, balanced colour that can add a sense of history or even approachability to a design. A great choice for heritage brands or those connected to the outdoors.

145

Deep Grey An easy neutral that will work across all palettes. A more mousey grey will pick up on some of the attributes of brown, whilst a clearer, sharper grey will feel more sophisticated. Very easy to make work in print and a good foil for many different palettes.

TYPOGRAPHY

Fonts, lettering, typefaces: whatever you call them, they can make a dramatic difference to the impact of your brand identity. Look beyond the 'system fonts' that came pre-installed on your computer and you'll find an exciting array of fonts with personality and style, ready to represent your business with flair.

Understanding how to choose type with intention, selecting fonts that communicate your brand values and business personality, and that balance out your colour palette and other brand elements can be game-changing.

In this chapter, we're going to source a well-balanced palette of typefaces that will engage your audience, set the right tone for your business and create a strong and distinctive look.

A GUIDE TO TYPEFACES

One of the most exciting things about sourcing fonts is the sheer variety and quality of what's available. From quirky, hand drawn lettering to solid, dependable sans serifs; from a curvaceous ball end serif to a flamboyant script font there is a font for every quirk, characteristic and idiosyncrasy.

Once you start looking closely at the design of a font you'll start to see how small details communicate subtle personality traits. Compare two very similar fonts closely and you'll find that they have very different things to 'say' about your business. This can be a fun, inspirational and slightly addictive part of the design process.

Let's start by looking at the major groups of typefaces and then we can delve a little deeper into their idosyncracies.

OLD SCHOOL We may source our fonts digitally now but these typebooks, owned by my father-in-law, traditional signwriter Paul Humberstone, are a rich source of inspiration and beauty,

BECOME A FONT AFICIONADO

Font fanatics can spend hours looking for a
typeface that's just so; one that balances the right
characteristics and style with the brief. Keep your
eyes on the major font foundaries and get into the
habit of saving or bookmarking fonts that you love.

SERIF

Serif fonts add a touch of elegance and traditionalism to a brand identity. The serifs are the 'bits' at the end of each letter and date back to Roman times when the serif was used to aid the stone masons in chiseling out the letters.

Serifs can certainly give your brand identity a heritage look, but when combined with contemporary colours and styling they can also look ultra modern. The editorial style that has become so popular is a great example of combining serif fonts with letterspacing to achieve a highly desirable and upmarket look.

SEMI SERIF

Semi serifs have, as the name suggests, less pronounced serifs that give them a less formal and more contemporary look. A useful style for a forward-thinking, professional services firm.

ball terminal or ball end serif

Ball terminal or ball end serifs add a touch of friendliness and approachability to this sometimes formal and aloof typeface. The terminals certainly add femininity to a typeface palette and could be balanced by a strong colour and condensed font if you were concerned about going too girly.

SLAB SERIF

Slab serifs bring substance and a certain masculinity to the traditional serif typeface. They contrast well with the feminine ball end serif and are currently used by companies wishing to display their ethical, authentic values.

SANS SERIF

Sans serif fonts are, by their very nature, modern and contemporary. They add a streamlined, clean and forward-thinking touch to your identity.

149

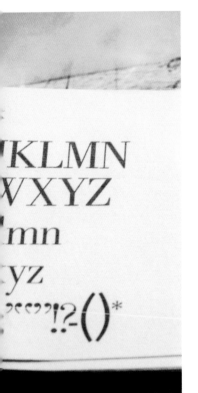

script

Script fonts bring personality and character to your brand identity. And from retro cool to elegant calligraphy there is a script font for every business. Use sparingly for the greatest effect.

display

Typefaces influenced by vintage typewriters, dymo labels and the art of paper cutting have gained popularity in recent years and are overwhelmingly hot right now. Typewriter fonts can add a pretty, vintage charm, whilst label and paper-cutting fonts add a quirky, handmade and contemporary edge.

Display fonts are fun to use and will certainly give your identity a very on-trend feel. Be careful to keep them at the edge of your identity however: as accent fonts rather than within your logo. They will fall from grace as fast as they found fame and will very quickly date your brand identity.

Handwriting

Handwritten typefaces add a lovely energy to a brand identity, literally infusing a personality into your brand and are well worth including in your type palette. Look at the energy in the script: some are slow and languidly written, others bursting with life and creativity. Some are spiky and sharp, whilst others are open and welcoming. Choose a style that speaks to you and that brings another dimension to your computer-generated scripts.

Hand Lettering

Sometimes, nothing can be more personal or appropriate than using your own handwriting. And if you have lovely handwriting then you're certainly guaranteed something unique!

There are a number of apps and online resources that will let you convert your writing into a typeface or simply import your pre-written phrases into Illustrator and use the Live Trace tool to create a useable vector file.

FONTS TO AVOID

There are a handful of fonts that have a bad press amongst professional designers; Comic Sans, Arial, Verdana, Times New Roman, Trebuchet and Papyrus are at the top of the list.

Some lack finesse, others have been woefully over-used, or mis-used and many are simply avoided due to plain, old-fashioned snobbery. And you need to avoid them too.

There are so many other fonts available to you that will add character, personality and style. Many of these fonts are very low cost, some are even free.

Obviously with email you're very limited and you're going to have to stick to one of the more common typefaces, that's OK, just add colour and your logo for an element of style and flair.

DELICIOUSLY WHOLESOME

An elegant typography palette, a splash of hand lettering and mouthwatering photography really brings The Medicinal Meal Plan's business to life. Yum!

TYPOGRAPHY

HOW TO USE TYPE LIKE A PRO

Choosing a great set of fonts will get you a long way, but how you use the type also matters. If you're serious about creating a stylish and dynamic identity, then it's worth learning some of the typography tricks that professional designers employ. You'll lift your communications to a whole new level.

THE ART OF TYPOGRAPHY

I've deliberately kept things simple here so that you can create a fabulous-looking identity without getting lost in jargon, but if you find yourself getting hooked, you'll find suggestions for further reading on page 203.

LEADING

The space between the lines of text. Add in space to create a feeling of lightness and airiness and make your body copy easier to read. Too little will make your text look dense and overwhelming, whilst too much can be difficult to read. Play around until you find a balance.

KERNING

The space between the letters. Also known as tracking or letterspacing. Add in to create elegance and grace or (when used with a condensed font), impact.

Decrease the kerning to create a bold statement. Best kept to logos and heading treatments, as it can be difficult to read body copy that's been kerned.

POINT SIZE

Make a statement by going smaller or larger than you naturally would. Many designers will use around 9-11pt text for body copy and around 14pt for the web. This is probably considerably smaller than you would expect and will really add a polished and professional finish to your designs.

WEIGHT

Fonts usually come in a variety of weights. For example, Light, Ultralight or Bold. Where possible, avoid Regular and instead use, say, a Light or Bold which will provide a more stylish and unusual finish.

You'll also need to consider practicalities. Hairline or Ultralight fonts will be difficult to reproduce in small sizes but can look fabulous as headers. To be sure that what you've designed is practical, print out your mock-up to spot anything that isn't right.

CAPTURING ALL
OF LIFE'S
LITTLE MOMENTS
AS THEY UNFOLD

TONIEDGEPHOTOGRAPHY.COM

TONI EDGE
PHOTOGRAPHY

PLEASE DELIVER TO

TONI EDGE PHOTOGRAPHY

TONIEDGEPHOTOGRAPHY.COM

TONIEDGEPHOTOGRAPHY@GMAIL.COM

Nikon

WORDS AND PICTURES Clean type, striking images and an uplifting yet restrained colour palette combine to create a strong, simple and effective brand identity for Californian photographer, Toni Edge. Diagonal lines add a feeling of movement and capture the essence of Toni's emphasis on creative spontaneity.

CONTRAST

Contrast is a key trick employed by professional designers to make things both easier to read and more beautiful. The key here is contrast, Light with Black will make a bigger statement than Regular with Bold. A Condensed font with a Light Italic. Large with Small, Slab with Sans etc.

HIERARCHY

Working out what matters most and giving each element a strict hierarchy will make all the difference to both the impact and professionalism of your designs. This is especially important in complex designs such as a website, brochure or leaflet, but just as relevant with a simple business card where you need to be able to find key information quickly. Ask yourself: 'What do people

154

need to know first, second and third?' And arrange and size your information accordingly.

COLUMN WIDTH

Or, more technically, the measure. This denotes the width of column that you can comfortably read before the eye gets tired. Too narrow and your message won't flow, too long and your reader will become fatigued. As a general rule 40-80 characters is considered ideal.

PAGE MARGINS

Wide page margins will give a more designed, less word-processed look to your documents. Take a look through books at home for examples.

YOUR LOGO FONT

Your logo should be distinctive and strong and for that reason it's important that you don't use the font from your logo anywhere else.

When you use the same font for your headings as you have in your logo, the strength of your logo is weakened and it starts to look a little like someone has just typed out your company name, which is definitely not the look we are going for.

IGNITING WONDER
Breathtaking photography and a textured, evocative brand identity has quickly established Mozell as a storyteller of adventure.

CHOOSING FONTS FOR YOUR BRAND

A considered and curated typeface 'palette' is an essential part of a well-styled brand. Contrasting and complementary fonts will give your brand identity energy, character and style and will ensure that your communications are both engaging and easy to understand.

Typically you'll need to select two or three font families for brand identity in addition to your logo font. You may find that if you blog a lot, you can use a few more. But given that fonts have so many different weights and variations, two or three is often enough.

THE ESSENTIALS

A font for your **logo** and one for your **strapline**. You won't use this font anywhere else.

A font for **headlines.** Your heading font will need to work well with your body copy font and can be, but doesn't need to be, from the same family. If you do choose a different font, make it intentional. If your body copy is a sans serif, go for a serif or slab serif to add some contrast and style.

A font for **body copy.** This needs to be legible when small and work in swathes of text, so a neat serif or sans serif font will work best here.

At least one **accent font** that you can use perhaps for client testimonials, perhaps to emphasise something on your packaging or on an image over a blog post. Consider a hand-drawn script or display font here to add plenty of style and personality.

WHAT DO YOU NEED?

Flick back through your scrapbook or journal (see pages 88-89) to the board you put together with your marketing communications and make a note of the font styles you anticipate you might need. If you're launching a new business it's worth imagining the sorts of material you might create in the future. What might you use?

Will you create images for your blog posts overlaid with beautiful typography? Perhaps you plan on producing books, downloadable PDFs or videos? Do you create proposals? How do you see these being structured?

Don't worry about going into too much detail at this point. Just get the broad elements in place before going back and fine-tuning the details later.

LOOK AND FEEL

You'll probably have a good idea from working through the briefing exercises in Chapter Two, **Planning** and the vision board process in Chapter Three, **Create Your Vision** as to what typefaces you're going to need. How should they look and feel?

Before you start sourcing, it's worth making a few notes on what you're aiming for: it'll help you stay focused in the face of creative overwhelm. How would you describe how you'd like each to feel?

Perhaps you're looking for a stylish, editorial, feminine font for your headings? You might team that with a modern, crisp and elegant font for your body copy and an engaging, cursive handwritten font for accents.

Alternatively you might be going for a more understated, contemporary and cool look with a strong sans serif combined with a slab serif for your body copy and script font to add contrast and personality.

Have fun experimenting with different options. It can be fun to see how each typeface brings something different to the party and how swapping in different styles can totally change the mood of a palette.

When you start to really look at typefaces you'll notice that each has its own personality that can add depth and style.

Look closely at the details: the way the serifs work, the shapes of the vowels, the finish of the dots and you'll start to see your brand identity really coming to life.

RESEARCHING

When you're sourcing fonts it's inspiring to look at some of the major font foundaries online. You'll find a list of my favourites in Resources (see p205). Some will have the option to create an album for your project so that you are able to save fonts that you respond to all in one place.

It's a good idea to not overthink the first stage. Allow yourself complete creative freedom and bookmark, pin or save fonts that you think might work. You can cull later, but initially you need some choice.

Have at the back of your mind the sorts of fonts you're looking for, but mostly just enjoy the creative freedom to explore. You search for fonts by keywords, so try putting one of your brand values into the search box and seeing what comes up.

You can also cross search on many of the sites. If you see a font that you quite like, look at the tags and see if any of these bring up something more interesting for you.

SHORTLISTING

You're going to shortlist your fonts in very much the same way you did your colours and also the images for your mood board. Start with a quick work through and ask yourself: 'What does this font say about my business?'

Next, look closely at the detail. What is the font saying to you? How does it feel? What character and personality will it bring?

Look at the practicalities. What weights does the font come in? For body copy you will need a normal, bold and italic weight at the very minimum. Are special characters such as question marks and currency signs included? They often aren't in free or unusual typefaces, and there is nothing worse than being on a deadline with your first proposal and realising that you can't complete the pages because you're missing a vital dollar sign.

PIECING TOGETHER YOUR SELECTION

How do all of your font choices work together? You're looking to create a balanced selection, so whilst you need some energy and personality in your palette, you'll need to temper that with a selection of more simple fonts for your body copy and perhaps for your headers too.

Whilst hand drawn or display fonts can be lovely, it is possible to have too much of a good thing. In general, one or two on the page will be plenty. Any more and they will all be shouting for attention and you'll struggle to be taken seriously.

Do the typefaces communicate the message you're looking for? What you'll hopefully find is that you're able to bring out different aspects of your brand personality with different fonts. Perhaps mixing a solid, efficient and reliable body copy font with a handwritten typeface with a touch of whimsy to add lightness and flair to your design.

Once you've made your final choices you can download and install your fonts on your computer ready for use. You'll need them for your brand board, if not sooner.

BLENDING THE OLD WITH THE NEW This brand identity by Caava Design for Californian Distillery Old Harbour makes maximum use of the mood and texture that can be evoked through considered use of type. Icons that give a nod to the name of the brand further add to the compelling nature of this design.

158

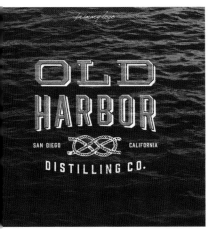

CHOOSING TYPEFACES THAT WILL SUPPORT YOUR BUSINESS VALUES

Once you start looking at type, the choices can become quite overwhelming. There must be tens of thousands of fonts available and creating a strong, cohesive look can be a challenge.

Be guided in the first instance by your colour psychology personality. This will narrow the field considerably and make the shortlisting much easier. Each season has a very distinctive style, and once you understand how that works, pulling together a coherent look suddenly becomes easier.

When you're planning on combining two seasons, typefaces are the ideal place to mix things up a little. So if your colours are rooted in summer but you want to bring a little winter edginess, now is the time to pull out the dramatic, editorial style fonts or the super-thin styles. Keep your colour palette rooted in summer and it'll all work really well.

FONTS FOR EVERY SEASONAL PERSONALITY

Spring typefaces are fine-featured and fun. Think Sans Serif, lighthearted hand drawn Display fonts and quirky, fun Scripts.

If you're looking for summer fonts, consider traditional Serif styles – perhaps keeping the look contemporary with plenty of leading or kerning and flowing, romantic Script or Handwriting fonts.

Autumn fonts are substantial, well-read and full of character. Slab Serifs, chunky, textured Handwriting or hand drawn fonts also work really well.

Finally, winter's extreme personality can take a very understated Sans Serif: add some drama with condensed, very light or very bold versions; add character with an over-the-top Handwriting font or an opulent and confident Serif.

RELAXED AND RECYCLED I love everything about this brand identity for Rewined Candles: from the packaging concept to the hand lettering that features on the pattern. Take a look at page 168 for the rest of the story.

160

DEFINING YOUR HOUSE STYLE

Create a mock-up of a document you use a lot: perhaps a proposal, report or invoice, and start to play around with your typefaces, styles and perhaps even your colours. You'll very quickly start to see what works and what doesn't.

If you're using Adobe InDesign for this, you can also create Paragraph Styles which you can then use to streamline your design process in the future.

As a rule, you'll need to create styles for at least: Heading One, Heading Two, Body Copy, Bullets and Numbering, and Emphasis.

BRAND ICONS AND DEVICES

Aside from your logo, icons and devices can add character and visual interest to your brand. Think about the sorts of collateral you may need to design for your marketing and communications. Are there any elements that would benefit from a set of icons to illustrate points, or parts of your process or offering that need specific sections defining?

Consider blog categories, services you offer or product categories. Would these benefit from icons? How about your social media icons on your website or blog: why not give them a style that fits with your brand identity.

Finally think about whether your business would benefit from a distinctive 'stamp' or icon that could be used alone on stickers, packaging or perhaps even at the bottom of your website to add visual interest and authenticity to your brand.

ENVIRONMENTALLY SOUND Organic patterns, rich colours and illustrations inspired by nature give this environmental consultancy a warm and authentic feel. Strong typography and directional devices keep things businesslike and demonstrate the company's commitment to their vision.

PRIMARY LOGO

Veris

TRULY SUSTAINABLE
GROWTH STRATEGIES

PRIMARY ILLUSTRATIONS

COLOUR PALETTE

MANIFESTO

transforming
ENVIRONMENTAL
ASPIRATIONS INTO
REAL ACTIONS *&*
beautiful results

SECONDARY DEVICES

PRIMARY FONTS

Crimson Italic
ABCDEFGHIJKLMNOPQRSTUVWXYZ

ZNIKOMIT
ABCDEFGHIJKLMNOPQRSTUVWXYZ

PATTERNS & EXTENDED ICONS

ILLUSTRATIONS

Illustrations add an element of style, flair and character to your brand identity. Use them to literally illustrate a point, give your packaging some oomph or simply engage with your audience.

You'll probably have an idea of the type of illustrations that might work for you from both the work you did with your vision statement and also when you were planning typefaces. Some brand identities simply don't need illustrations and I certainly don't recommend you create them for the sake of it, but when done well, they can add a lovely sparkle.

As with the other elements of your brand identity, the styling matters, so choose a style that fits with your seasonal personality. For a spring business that means perhaps a characterful and clean illustrative style with fine lines and movement.

A summer illustration style would have a more drifting quality to it, with perhaps ink and watercolour adding definition and texture. An autumnal illustrative style would have substance: bold, hand drawn lines perhaps or smoother, cleaner and simple shapes with plenty of body. Winter illustrations will be arresting: a strong, characterful style that's instantly recognisable.

If you're a confident artist, this is your time to let your skills shine. Brainstorm what you might draw: depending on how and where you plan to use your illustrations and enjoy creating.

Remember you can always trace from photographs if you don't feel comfortable drawing freehand. Your drawing style is unique and can add a lovely personal touch to your brand identity.

BOTANICALLY SPEAKING Bath-based letterpress and design studio Meticulous Ink created this breathtakingly beautiful brand identity for a new florist in the city. Quite literally drawing their inspiration from the floral product, the result feels elegant and very much in touch with nature.

PATTERN AND TEXTURE

A well-curated collection of both pattern and textures is often the difference between a well-styled and distinctive brand identity and just a logo and a set of fonts. Patterns add character, distinction and an element of style and consistency.

Consider using a mixture of stripes, dots, illustrations or geometric shapes to add impact and diversity. Your patterns will consolidate the message you're sending out about your business and create atmosphere.

If you have the skills, it can be fun to create your own patterns. There are plenty of really good online resources and books that will guide you through the process of creating a pattern that will tile, or repeat, seamlessly. Take a look in Resources (page 203) for some of my favourites.

Use your own illustrations or perhaps your brand icons to create 'wallpaper' that you can take to exhibitions, use as wrapping or even put in the background of your blog.

Photoshop and Illustrator both have a great selection of brushes that will enable you to quickly and easily create simple patterns: stripes, dots, paint spatters, watercolour marks or texture for example and there are plenty more that can be downloaded online. It's a fun and inspiring creative process, so treat yourself to a little time for experimenting if you can.

For those of us without the time, confidence or inclination to create our own patterns, there is a great selection of stock patterns available at very low cost. Pattern is definitely something that you can source online, and then personalise by adapting the colour palette to suit your unique identity.

WHIPPING UP A STORM Talented chef and socially conscious entrepreneur Alli commissioned Serafini Creative to design an identity that reflects the essence of her food. Simple and iconic illustrations, bold pattern and natural kraft paper combine for an understated but confident look.

PULLING TOGETHER AN EXCEPTIONAL PATTERN PALETTE

Play with scale Mix small, delicate pieces with larger, more dramatic patterns to add movement and texture within your palettes.

Mix and match Pull together different styles for diversity and character. Stripes, florals, dots, geometric shapes and illustrative pattern. All mix well when grounded with a common colour palette.

Create texture as well as scale Use colour and pattern styles to create movement, drama and texture in your pattern palette.

Go with your gut Do you love it? Then the chances are it's probably right for your brand.

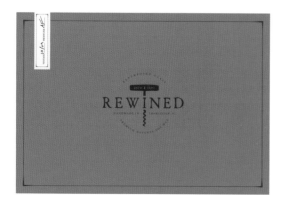

SELECTING PATTERNS TO SUPPORT YOUR BRAND

As you might expect, just as you can use your seasonal personality to source fonts and colours that will send out the right signals about your brand, you can also apply the same process to your patterns.

Pattern is a great area to deliberately pull in elements from your subordinate season and create something truly unique. Just make sure that you remember to use the colour palette from your core season.

For example, if you have a business that is the winter side of spring, your colour palette will be rooted in spring (light, bright and clear) but you might incorporate some more defined, geometric patterns and strong stripes to give your brand a more grown-up, aspirational look. This is brand styling at its best: intentional, creative and stylish.

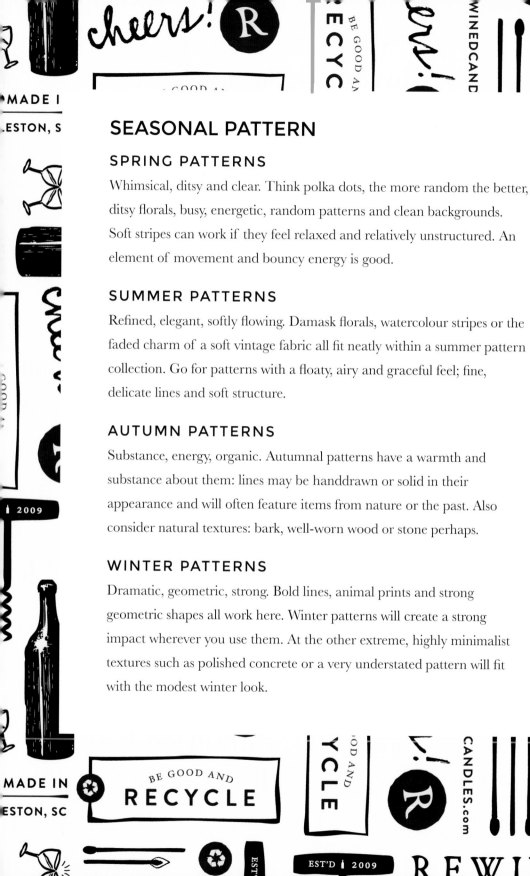

SEASONAL PATTERN

SPRING PATTERNS

Whimsical, ditsy and clear. Think polka dots, the more random the better, ditsy florals, busy, energetic, random patterns and clean backgrounds. Soft stripes can work if they feel relaxed and relatively unstructured. An element of movement and bouncy energy is good.

SUMMER PATTERNS

Refined, elegant, softly flowing. Damask florals, watercolour stripes or the faded charm of a soft vintage fabric all fit neatly within a summer pattern collection. Go for patterns with a floaty, airy and graceful feel; fine, delicate lines and soft structure.

AUTUMN PATTERNS

Substance, energy, organic. Autumnal patterns have a warmth and substance about them: lines may be handdrawn or solid in their appearance and will often feature items from nature or the past. Also consider natural textures: bark, well-worn wood or stone perhaps.

WINTER PATTERNS

Dramatic, geometric, strong. Bold lines, animal prints and strong geometric shapes all work here. Winter patterns will create a strong impact wherever you use them. At the other extreme, highly minimalist textures such as polished concrete or a very understated pattern will fit with the modest winter look.

PHOTOGRAPHY

As you've seen from many of the inspirational examples in this book, photography plays a huge role in your brand identity. From your website and blog to packaging, stationery, marketing literature and everything in-between, images that capture the essence of your business are a real asset to your brand.

When selecting a photographer, look closely at their portfolio, looking at both what their style is and also the types of images they prefer to shoot.

Take your cues from your seasonal personality. Spring images will be fun, colourful, light and bright. They'll have a softness about them and a certain warmth.

Conversely summer images will be cooler, calmer and more relaxed. This is the time for a well-placed lens flare or hazy, lazy light. Again, images will have a softness about them.

Colours in autumn photography will be rich, intense and very often natural in feel. They'll have an energy about them that's very motivating.

Winter photography may be crisp, clean, bright, intense and clear or the total opposite: grounded, understated and edgy. Either way, expect winter images to provoke a strong emotive reaction.

Enjoy the process: beautiful photographs really unlock your creativity and transform your design.

STORYTELLING Evocative photography and a beautifully elegant use of type makes this website design for photographers Joe and Patience thoroughly compelling. The collection of heirloom books, photographic equipment and weathered textures tell an especially powerful story that connects directly with the visitor.

BRINGING EVERYTHING TOGETHER WITH CONFIDENCE AND PURPOSE

There is something so exciting about collecting together each of your brand elements and seeing how they work as a whole. This is your chance to see the full impact of your hard work, assess what works, what doesn't and how the whole brand identity fits together.

Expect to tweak things, throw things out and start again and you will produce a better brand identity for it. In fact, actively look for what's not working and opportunities to improve what you've done, that's where the magic happens.

WORKING UP THE CONCEPTS

As well as creating a brand board (more on that over the page), it's worth designing a couple of pieces of collateral to see how your design will work in practice. For example, you might mock up a business card, a slide for a presentation, or a simple piece of packaging. Maybe see how the brand would look as signage, or on the side of your vehicle. Whatever brings your identity to life and, most importantly, test out whether you like where you've got to.

PREPARING FOR FEEDBACK

If you're designing your own brand identity, it's quite likely that you'll want to send your ideas to some trusted friends and colleagues for feedback. Rather than just sending across your brand board, consider including a paragraph or two on your brief and objectives for the redesign as well as why your concept answers the brief. It's a good discipline for you (to be sure that it does), but it also goes a long way to preventing the unhelpful feedback that revolves around subjective opinion rather than the relevance of what you've done.

Mōzell

_Mō_

IGNITE WONDER   LEE@MOZELLFILMS.COM   443.392.8773   MOZELLFILMS.COM
5004 HONEYGO CENTER DRIVE, SUITE 102-154
PERRY HALL MARYLAND 21128

Mōzell

MOZELLFILMS.COM

LEE MORTON

CREATIVE DIRECTOR
LEAD EXPLORER

LEE@MOZELLFILMS.COM
443.392.8773

THE SPIRIT OF ADVENTURE Packed
with energy and a sense of wonder, this
striking brand identity for Mozell films
really comes to life in the stationery
mockups created by Braizen. Quirky
business cards and printed envelopes
make an instant impact.

BRINGING EVERYTHING TOGETHER

BRAND BOARDS
AND BRAND BOOKS

Brand boards serve a far greater purpose than simply providing graphic designers with something visual to share on Pinterest or Behance. They are an instant visual reference and give you the opportunity to review where you're at. This is your chance to make sure that your brand identity has the depth and personality you set out to create at the beginning of this process.

As you work through each element of styling your brand, it's easy to lose sight of your achievements: both in terms of how far you've come and also your original vision. If the mood board is your jumping-off point, then your brand board is your checkpoint.

As you collate all of your brand elements in one place you'll be able to spot very easily how the brand identity works as a whole and whether there are any gaps to be filled. Does your heart sing or sink? Are you smiling at how fabulous it all looks together (I do hope so!) or do you see some room for improvement?

Once you have everything in place, pull out your mood board and your original brief and ask yourself: 'Does this achieve what I set out to?' If not, are you happy with where it's at, or do you need to make some refinements?

Styling a brand is addictive and it's something that becomes very easy to spend a lot of time tinkering with over and over again. Putting together a brand board, or if you have the time, a brand book, is a nice full stop to the process. Share it on your blog, print it out poster size and have it framed for your studio wall. Better still, have it make into a hardback book so that you can really celebrate all that you've achieved.

CLEAN LINES Working up designs is all part of the brand styling process for Making Waves Creative. It's easy to see how effectively the various colours, patterns, fonts and devices combine to create a fresh, striking look for career coach Rikke Hansen.

174

HOW TO PUT TOGETHER A BRAND BOOK

A brand manual, style guide or brand book is an essential way of ensuring that your brand identity is implemented consistently across all of your marketing literature.

Keep it close at hand and share it with your team and associates, as well as any graphic or web designers who may work on your business. They are time consuming but fun to put together and are well worth the effort!

As well as your brand elements you'll want to add some detail on the company, your vision and values, the creative brief, colour palette, mood board and guidelines on how to use the brand identity. I'd also recommend you include any design work so that you always have a reference for the design style.

ABCD
abcdefghijklm
nopqrstuvwxyz
1234567890

ABCD
ABCDEFGHIJKLM
NOPQRSTUVWXYZ
1234567890

ABCD
abcdefghijklmnopqrstuvwxyz
1234567890

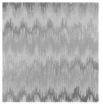

BOHO-CHIC This luxurious brand identity for event-design company Plush, based in Doha-Qatar, creates a distinctive and colourful splash. Bold pattern, geometric shapes and touches of spring energy capture the fun and celebratory nature of the company.

EVALUATING CREATIVE WORK

Whether you have styled your own brand or are working with a talented designer, it's important to have a structured process for reviewing your creative work. And whilst your initial gut reaction is an important one, so is taking a more objective and considered approach.

Allow time for this process: for reviewing and reflecting as well as refining and tweaking to ensure that what's ultimately produced has longevity and is right for your business.

Those of you who have outsourced your design will find that it is much easier to objectively evaluate the work your designer has produced if it's not your own blood, sweat and tears that have gone into the design.

Evaluating your own work requires discipline and a commitment to excellence. It can be a testing and sometimes painful process for even the most perfectionist of us. I'd suggest you work through this stage with a couple of trusted business friends who are supportive and also bring the right level of challenge.

FIVE ESSENTIAL QUESTIONS FOR REVIEWING CREATIVE WORK

1

How does each element meet the brief? If you've followed the process in this book closely, you'll find that your finished work will be very close to your original intent. But we are all susceptible to magpie tendencies and if you've drifted creatively a long way from your original intention, now is a good time to notice this.

Go back to your brief and remind yourself of your three key words: how does each element support these aims? Be honest with yourself. If something doesn't support your brand message, question whether the brief needs to change or your design. Work out how to either bring your design back on track or realign your business vision to fit your creative style.

2

Does this reflect what we set out to achieve? Does what you've produced live up to the big vision that you created at the outset? If it doesn't, be prepared to commit a little more time to create something truly exceptional.

3 **Do I like how this fits together?** How cohesive does your brand identity look as a whole? When it looks right, stop. Over time your brand may evolve, but you also need to know when to stop or you will never get any work done. Once your brand identity looks and feels right, accept that you are finished and move on.

4 **Does this feel right?** Your brand identity should make your heart sing and your spirits soar. It should bring a smile to your face and make you proud to be associated with it. If you're not feeling like that, break down each element and ask yourself what you can tweak.

5 **Am I proud of this?** The key to styling your own brand is to make sure it doesn't look any less smart than if you'd paid a professional. Look closely at the details: the fonts you've used, the way things line up, is everything on point?

EMBRACING FEEDBACK TO MAKE YOUR WORK EVEN BETTER

Critiques are an essential and highly positive part of any creative process. People not as close to the project as you will help you see things in a different light; they will boost your confidence and also encourage you in your quest to create a truly unique brand identity.

When you're in the middle of styling a brand it can seem that everyone has an opinion: whether they are qualified to have one or not. Working out who to listen to can be difficult, because sometimes the loudest, most persuasive people are not the ones who have the most relevant opinions.

NAVIGATING THE MINEFIELD OF FEEDBACK

It matters that your current and prospective profitable clients love what you've done, and we've worked through a pretty robust process to ensure that they do. Your team, associates and trusted business friends are also likely to understand your vision for your business and will have valid opinions (that's not to say you have to agree with them).

It matters considerably less that your partner, siblings, next door neighbour or brother's best friend's dog loves your brand identity.

Everyone will always have a view and you simply can't listen to everyone or you will land up with a design that pleases no one. You could end up losing the instinctive, emotional reaction that we've worked so hard to try and create.

Be confident in what you've done. Listen to the gems because you can learn from the feedback and make your work even better, but you can't, and won't, please them all.

FEEDING BACK TO YOUR DESIGNER

Send them a short note with your **gut reaction** (on the basis that it'll be a good one!) and then give yourself a good few days to digest what you have been presented with and to gather feedback.

Don't give them chapter and verse on all the feedback you've gained, work through the **headlines**.

Discuss rather than email so that you can gain the benefit of their advice and together work through the best route forwards.

Tell them what you love – we all like to know we've done a good job.

Be honest with what you don't, and really try and analyse why something isn't working for you. Use the notes on colour psychology to help you be objective and move forwards.

Remember that **changes are a natural part of the design process**. They help you get closer to something that's right for your unique business. Enjoy the journey.

DON'T LOVE WHAT YOU SEE?

Take a deep breath and resist the temptation to email them five pages with your disappointment.

Try and **remove the emotion** from the scenario. This isn't your fault, nor is it necessarily theirs. There has simply been a breakdown in communication. Ask yourself how your brief has been misinterpreted, what you were expecting and if there is anything that can be done to rectify the situation.

Sleep on it You may have a change of heart.

Don't be nervous Most designers want to create something you will love. Be honest, explain what you don't like, try and pick a few things that you do. and try and work out a route forward.

As long as you picked the right designer in the first place (i.e. you loved their portfolio and felt a strong connection between the two of you) this situation will be salvageable. **Be confident and enjoy the challenge** of creating something you truly love.

CHAPTER SIX

STYLING IT UP

"BE SO GOOD
THEY CAN'T IGNORE YOU."
- STEVE MARTIN

CREATE A SPLASH

Your brand identity is complete! Time to get it out there to start winning you business.

Throughout this book I've shared examples of small businesses applying their brand identities with style and panache to their packaging, stationery and websites. I hope it's inspired you to think about the possibilities for your own business.

What follows are the absolute essentials you need to know to style up your brand with confidence.

HOW TO CREATE A BUSINESS CARD WITH IMPACT

Whatever you do for a living, your business card is probably your most essential piece of kit. It's the one thing we all use, whether you're a prolific networker or you prefer to spend most of your working day in your studio. A great business card will open up opportunities, provide a talking point and will certainly make you, and your business, memorable.

When you've had a great conversation with someone, isn't it lovely to hand over a card that really makes a positive impression? Create a splash with a unique hand finish, a pop of pattern or an illustration that creates a talking point. Here's how.

186

1 PLAY WITH SCALE
Your cards don't need to be politely ordered and quiet. Have fun with hand lettering or paint to create a splash!

2 HAND FINISH FOR A PERSONAL TOUCH
Surely a must-do if you're in a crafty creative industry? Think washi tape, hand or machine stitching or embellishments that add personality and character.

3 INVEST IN SOMETHING DIFFERENT
Think letterpress, embossing, foil blocking or edge painting your cards to create instant wow factor.

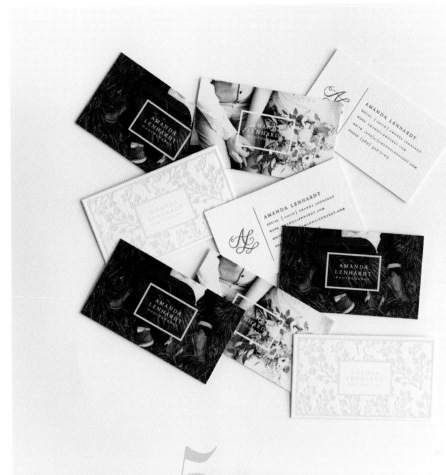

5 STAMP IT

And be imaginative with what you stamp onto: kraft card, fabric or even plastic can work with the right tools.

4 USE THE BACK TO ADD IMPACT

Add patterns, quotes illustrations, block colour, or photographs to show off your work and create a talking point.

6 GET CREATIVE WITH THE FORMAT

Think cut-out, folded, pop-up or punched. And who says business cards have to be rectangular?

THE ABSOLUTE ESSENTIALS OF
BUSINESS CARD DESIGN

Less is more when it comes to creating an impact Pare information back to the essentials: certainly your name, company name, email address and website address. Ask yourself what else you need? A telephone number is usual but by no means essential, particularly if you prefer to be contacted via email. Keep social media profiles for your website and avoid QR codes to keep things clutter free.

Think in terms of creating three sections usually your logo and strapline; your name and job title and finally your contact details. Cluster information together to make your card easy to use and a pleasure to look at.

Keep the font small but legible around 8-9pt is usually ideal, preferably no larger than 10pt unless you work with a group of clients you know have poor eyesight.

Try and find a way of aligning at least two of the elements to bring an element of cohesion and style.

Where possible, **create a visual link to the reverse** Wrap a colour around slightly, give a hint of a pattern, anything to intrigue!

Business cards usually have a finished size of 85 x 55mm or 50 x 90mm finished size in the US. There's no reason yours needs to conform to those dimensions if you don't want it to, but it's nice to know where you're starting from. Add around 1.5mm 'bleed' to each edge (ask your printer for advice) to allow for cutting and trimming and take your pattern or colour right up to this line. Leave a gap of around 5mm from each edge for any vital text: this allows your design to look balanced and professional.

Business cards are usually **printed on thick stock**: anything from 300gsm up to a very chunky 600gsm. The thicker the better

FRESH FROM THE PLOT These mouthwatering veggies, commissioned by Viewers Like You and illustrated by Marta Spendowska take centre stage in the marketing materials and website of internationally acclaimed holistic health coach Holli Thompson. The brief called for a fluid look, with lots of juice and vibrancy — the perfect collaboration for Marta, who is in love with the glorious, capricious nature of watercolour.

LUCKY LAB COFFEE CO
AUSTIN, TEXAS

Lucky Lab Coffee Co is a mobile coffee bar run by entrepreneurs-with-a-conscience Ron Lunan and Courtney Hutton. The husband-and-wife team commissioned Braizen to create a vintage but clean brand identity that referenced their four beloved dogs.

A pared-back colour palette, natural textures, a strong use of typography and clean, hand drawn icons create a look that's as alluring as the foodie treats within the van.

PRIMARY LOGO

SECONDARY LOGO

COLOR PALETTE

BRAND ICONS

SIMPLIFIED LOGO

LUCKY LAB COFFEE CO

WATERMARKS / STAMPS

BRAND TYPOGRAPHY

Knockout Liteweight

Eames Century Modern

Gotham Book

TAGLINES

PURVEYORS OF HANDCRAFTED COFFEE

WET NOSES • WARM HANDS • HOT COFFEE

PATTERNS & TEXTURES

HOW TO CREATE A WEBSITE THAT SELLS

However you plan on creating your website, whether you've already booked a top agency or will pull something together yourself from a template, preparation is everything. There's a lot to consider when creating a powerful website for your business, too much to go into here, but I hope that the guidance below stands you in good stead. Whoever you work with, it's all about the planning and focus.

Time to pull out that notebook, take yourself off somewhere quiet and get thinking.

1 START WITH THE END IN MIND

What do you want this website to do? How will you know it's a success? Consider how successful your current website is and what your goals are for the new site.

2 WHAT DO YOU WANT PEOPLE TO KNOW, THINK AND DO?

How should your visitors feel when they arrive on your site? What do they need to know about your business? What do you want to tell them?

Having a clear idea of what information you want on your website and how you'd like it to be structured is essential if you're to get the best out of your investment. Make a note of the pages you think you need for your website and revise this as you work through the questions below. Even if you plan on having a one-page website, you still need to view each 'section' as a page and treat it the same way. For each page, ask yourself, 'What should people know, think and do?'

3 HOW WILL YOUR CUSTOMERS JOURNEY THROUGH YOUR SITE?

Think about your sales journey. If you want people to book you for their wedding, they're unlikely to do that via a PayPal button on your website, it just doesn't work like that. So what you actually want is for people to enquire about your availability. What do they need to see in order to do that? What do they need to know? Knowing all of this means that you can structure your website in a way that makes sense to your prospective clients and make it easy for them to do business with you.

Think about the content you need to engage your clients, to get them excited about your product or service and ultimately, to get them to take action. Make notes, create mind maps or spider diagrams and sketch out thoughts for banners or buttons that compel people to take action.

4 DO YOUR RESEARCH

Who in your industry is doing this well? Take a look at the websites of your competitors. What can you learn from them? Ask yourself: 'What's our take on this?' and 'How can we differentiate ourselves?' Use this as a chance to create something even better. Look at what isn't working as well as what is. Make notes, copious notes and learn from what you see.

FRESH AND CLEAN Well planned, beautifully photographed and thoughtfully designed, the Northernly website was built on a template customised by owner Kerry Pauly. Armed with beautiful images and a professionally designed logo the finished article is clean and highly polished.

5 WHO ARE YOU TALKING TO?

One of the hardest, and most powerful, things you can do when writing any copy or creating any piece of marketing literature is to visualise specific clients. Think back to the work we did on customer archetypes in Chapter Two, **Planning** and put yourself in their shoes. What do they need or want and how does your business help them? Really understand this from your clients' perspective and you'll find the words will flow.

6 CREATE CONTENT THAT ENGAGES YOUR VISITORS

It's not all about the hard sell. Create content that draws people in, that helps them gain an understanding of your brand and enables you to start to build a relationship. That might be a look book, a 'how to' or specific featured content from your blog. But it's about more than just the blog, it's about giving people an insight into your world that feels more considered and less off-the-cuff than your blog might be. Do you create new collections every season? Show people how you got there. Share the journey, it'll sell your expertise and it'll spark interest.

8 WRITE COPY THAT SELLS

Take the time to be clear in your own mind about what you're selling, who you're selling it to and why they will want to buy it. Consider how to communicate that succinctly and in a way that makes people want to act.

7 CAPTURE DATA

Not everyone that visits your website is ready to buy or even make an enquiry. Make it worth their while joining your mailing list. What can you offer them? When you join mine, I promise captivating content, special offers from time to time and news on the book and future workshops. Make sure you ask people to join your list, give them a good reason to do so and of course, make sure you use the list! If you run an ecommerce business it's really worth considering a pop-up invitation – you'll see your sign-up rates increase dramatically.

TOP TIPS FOR

DESIGNING YOUR OWN WEBSITE

Keep it simple Unless you have superfab coding skills and are an experienced designer, it's best to keep the structure, design and functionality really simple and let your words and your brand identity shine. Less is very much more.

Start with a theme and customise it to suit your brand style. A well designed theme that can be adapted to suit your brand identity is a quick, cost effective and smart way to create a website when you're on a budget. Be sure to make it your own so that it doesn't undermine your professionalism.

Invest in beautiful imagery, it will create a strong first impression and lift the whole website.

Plan, plan, plan! Nothing beats taking the time to consider how your site is going to work commercially for you.

A MALIBU HOLIDAY
EXTRAVAGANZA

PASSED APPETIZERS

buttermilk brined fried chicken and waffles with sea salt butter and spiced maple-bacon
syrup

niman ranch beef burger sliders with hook's cheddar, sweet bread and butter pickles,
ketchup, and aioli

meyer lemon, sweet pea, and goat cheese arancini with calabrian chili aioli

SALAD COURSE

market lettuces with citrus, castelvetrano olive, citronette, niman ranch bacon, and
buttermilk

MAIN COURSE

herb-brined and roasted jidori

9 CREATE WIREFRAMES

Drawing up a set of wireframes is an essential part of creating or commissioning a powerful website. They help you to make sure that your site will have the commercial impact you need before you move on to the design stage.

Quite simply, wireframes are simple sketches of each page: usually with boxes showing where key information should go and which headlines go where. They help you organise where everything will go and make sure you've thought enough about how your clients will move through your website.

You might find, if you're outsourcing this, that your designer has a better suggestion for the layout, but they'll certainly be grateful for you putting the commercial thought in before they start on the creative work!

Once you've completed the planning work, take the time to map out the structure of your website and also a wireframe for each key page. Use your notes, from questions 2 and 3 in particular, to guide you.

WHOA NELLY! I'm a huge fan of vintage botanical illustrations and I love how this website for Whoa Nelly makes full use of the impact they create close up combined with a contemporary and simple logo design. The graphics at the top are used as rotating headers and make a strong impact upon landing on the site.

CREATE A LASTING IMPRESSION

Whether you're starting or growing a business, creating a compelling website and building an engaged social media tribe are likely to be at the top of your list.

And whilst I wholeheartedly recommend you embrace those channels, don't overlook the power of touch. Whilst your competitors are cutting costs by eschewing print, you have the chance to stand out and be memorable with a few smart moves.

Think about what you might produce as a pre-sale welcome pack to help you get ahead of the game. What can you mail your clients at the start of a project to reassure them they made the right choice with you?

Consider your packaging: unbranded mailing cartons hardly make a splash. Instead, customise with pattern and some copy that gets your recipient as excited as you are about your business.

And don't forget your invoice. Your last chance to make a lasting impression. Create something that's well designed and warm, something that will have your clients aching to do business with you again.

CLASSIC AND SIMPLE *Opposite* Californian graphic designer James Prunean has created an elegant brand identity and stand-out set of print collateral for his wife, Diana Marie, that really allows her photography to shine. The branded memory stick along with postcards of images from the day keep the experience going long after the project is complete.

GOOD ENOUGH TO EAT *Above* Thoughtful touches and attention to detail can make all the difference in our experience with a company. Here. Lucky Lab's cookies are wrapped in branded brown paper bags and secured with striped washi tape for a low-cost but high-impact presentation.

MOVING YOUR BRAND ON

Those of you that have been in business for a while will be all too aware of what I call 'magpie syndrome'. That ugly and oh-so frustrating habit of general dissatisfaction with your new brand identity within six months of your launch.

That grass-is-greener look over your shoulder that tells you that the knockout design you've just seen on your competitor's website is exactly what you need, can nurture an annoying desire to keep tinkering, tweaking refining. It's possible to keep borrowing inspiration from everything around you, until the point at which your brand identity has lost all focus and cohesion.

Well not this time. Things are different now.

TAMING YOUR INNER MAGPIE

We're all susceptible to magpie tendencies, but if you've followed this process, worked with a great brand stylist or worked hard yourself to produce something incredible, then you don't need to keep dabbling.

Unless your business is undergoing rapid change, or you're consistently getting feedback that your clients aren't seeing in your business what you had hoped for, then accept that your brand identity is doing its job, and move on.

Remember how you felt when you signed off your project? You made intelligent choices about every single element of your identity. You selected each aspect to appeal to a well-considered, profitable client profile. Don't let the day-to-day demands of running a business undermine your confidence in your choices. Make a pact with yourself that unless there is a genuine business reason to do so, you won't tinker with your branding for at least a year.

HOW OFTEN TO REBRAND?

Your brand is unlikely to date quickly, so unless you are changing direction dramatically, I'd suggest that you refresh the design of your website every two or three years, but that your core brand identity – colours and logo design – should work for you for around 10 years or more.

As part of your website refresh it's a good idea to update some of the peripheral elements of your brand identity: accent fonts perhaps, icons – anything that's highly fashionable when you launch that has dated fast. Simply refresh and move forwards. But don't keep tinkering!

WHAT NEXT?

We may be at the end of the book, but it's likely that your brand styling journey is just beginning. I hope that you'll use *How to Style Your Brand* as a resource throughout the process, to keep coming back to, like a trusted friend.

On my blog, **thebrand-stylist.com**, you'll find a wealth of resources I've created exclusively for you. You can download briefing forms, worksheets and the Brand Stylist Manifesto for your studio space. I'll be adding more over time, so do sign up to receive the latest updates.

Now that you have a complete overview of what's involved, you'll have a good idea of whether you are up for taking on the task yourself or will work with a designer. Whichever route you take, I wish you luck and lots of fun along the way.

Warmest,

Fiona

GLOSSARY

Throughout the book I've tried to avoid industry jargon but there are some terms that really are unavoidable. Here's the lowdown...

Brand Board A collection of all your brand elements: your logo, colour palette, typefaces, pattern and so on. See p26 for the full breakdown.

Mood Board Also referred to as a vision board. A collection of images, textures, patterns and so on that visually capture the essence of what you're trying to achieve. See p90.

Rule of thirds or the golden ratio. We respond best to things that are 'in proportion' and the rule of thids is a great way to ensure your design has balance. It's a complex subject but Wikipedia and Google are great sources of further information.

Wireframes are sketches that illustrate what's going where on your website. See p196.

RESOURCES

BOOKS

Exhibit! How to use Exhibitions to Grow Your Small Business
Fiona Humberstone, Copper Beech Press

Logo Design Love
David Airey, Peachpit Press

Logo Savvy
WOW! Branding, Rockport

The Beginners Guide To Colour Psychology
Angela Wright. Colour Affects

The Non-Designers Design Book
Robin Williams, Peachpit Press

WEBSITES

Design Seeds: An inspirational source for colour palettes *design-seeds.com*

The Brand Stylist: My blog, packed with inspirational examples, essential know how and my latest workshops and events. *thebrand-stylist.com*

ThemeForest My favourite source for Wordpress blog and website themes. *themeforest.com*

Creative Market. A marketplace packed with fonts, patterns and hand illustrated elements. Ideal for adding sparkle to your brand identity. *creativemarket.com*

Print & Pattern A blog that celebrates surface pattern design. A rich source of inspiration. *printpattern.blogspot.com*

My Fonts My very favourite resource for typefaces. Super easy to use and super inspiring. *myfonts.com*

Unsplash Achingly beautiful free stock photos with unlimited use. Very compelling. *unsplash.com*

Death to the Stock Photo ten free images a month. Light filled and cool. *deathtothestockphoto.com*

Veer Contemporary typefaces, illustrations, patterns and non-cheesy stock photos. *veer.com*

Butterick's Practical Typography A beautifully designed and immensely useful guide to typography. *practicaltypography.com*

Typography Deconstructed Insightful and thoroughly helpful guide to typography. *typographydeconstructed.com*

FEATURED DESIGNERS

This lovely lot have made the book what it is with their jaw-droppingly inspirational brand styling and creative genius. They also read like my go-to list for client projects, definitely worth talking to about your project.

Belinda Love Lee
belindalovelee.com

Braizen
getbraizen.com

Buttercup Ink
buttercupink.com

Caava Design
caavadesign.com

Cocorinna
cocorinna.com

Dilley & Jones
dilleyandjones.co.uk

Ditto
ditto.uk.com

Eva Black Design
evablackdesign.com

Grit & Wit
gritandwitdesign.com

James Prunean
jamesprunean.com

Jon King Design
jonkingdesign.com

Julie Song Ink
juliesongink.com

Lauren Ledbetter
laurenledbetter.com

Making Waves Creative
makingwavescreative.com

Meticulous Ink
meticulousink.com

Minna May
minnamay.com

Nothing But Lovely
nothingbutlovely.co.uk

Pinegate Road
pinegateroad.com

Pretty Unexpected
prettyunexpected.com

Rae Ann Kelly
raeannkelly.com

Revival Designbüro
revival-design.de

Rowan Made
rowanmade.com

Saffron Avenue
saffronavenue.com

Salted Ink Digital Design Co
saltedink.com

Serafini Creative
serafinicreative.com

Stitch Design Co
stitchdesignco.com

Studio 9
thestudio9company.com

Tonik
brandingbytonik.co.uk

Top Right Design
topright.co.uk

Very Marta
verymarta.com

Viewers Like You
viewers-like-you.com

We Are Branch
wearebranch.com

FEATURED PHOTOGRAPHERS

Super-talented creators of beautiful images. What's not to love?

Aline Bouma
paperboats.nl

Anne Almasy
annealmasy.com

Betsy Mobbs
mobbsphoto.wordpress.com

Brooke Schwab
brookeschwab.com

Chelsea Fullerton
goforthcreative.com

Diana Marie
dianamarieblog.com

Emily Quinton
makelight.io

Erin Witkowski
eveswishphotography.com

Gemma Williams
gemmawilliamsphotography.
co.uk

Jen Dillender
jendillenderphotography.com

Matt Pereira
mattpereira.co.uk

Mikaela Hamilton
mikaelahamilton.com

Peter Frank Edwards
pfephoto.com

Shay Cochrane
shaycochrane.com

Sully Sullivan Photography
ohsully.com

Vicki Knights
vickiknights.co.uk

Whitney Neal
whitneynealphoto.com

FEATURED BUSINESSES

Allison Sosna Group
chefallisosna.com

Amanda Lenhardt Photography
amandalenhardt.com

Arianna's Daily
ariannasdaily.com

Arthur Cottam
cottamhorseshoes.com

Bare Blooms
bareblooms.co.uk

Bayntun Flowers
bayntunflowers.co.uk

Blush Photography
photosbyblush.com

Bookishly
bookishly.co.uk

Career on Your Terms
careeronyourterms.com

Chimpanas
chinampas.co.uk

Clare Nolan
clarenolan.com

Commonplace Personal Goods
commonplaceshop.com

Edmund's Oast
edmundsoast.com

EnRoute Photography
enroutephotography.com

Finding Home
findinghomeonline.com

Floral Theory
floraltheory.com

Flowerona
flowerona.com

Given London
givenlondon.com

Grange Corner Farm
facebook.com/GrangeCornerFarm

Hannah Bergen
hannahbergen.com

Haute Chefs
hautechefsla.com

Hero
hero-online.co.uk

Holli Thompson
hollithompson.com

Hotel deWindketel
windketel.nl

I Heart Organizing
iheartorganizing.blogspot.com

JC Lemon
jclemon.com

Jill Smith
jillsmith.com

Joe & Patience
joeandpatience.com

Kate Whelan Events
katewhelanevents.com

Lenore Design
lenoredesign.com

Lisa Cox Garden Design
lisacoxdesigns.co.uk

Little Big Bell
littlebigbell.com

Little Shop of Brands
littleshopofbrands.com

Loaf
loaf.com

Lucends
lucends.com

Lucky Lab Coffee Co
luckylabcoffee.com

Maddie Hatton Food & Styling
maddiehatton.com

Manuela Bertol
manuelabertol.com.br

Maras Creative
marascreative.com

Medicinal Meal Plans
clairesholisticpursuits.com

Mozell
mozellfilms.com

Nathalie Marguez Courtney
nathalie.ie

Nectar and Green
nectarandgreen.com

Northernly
shopnorthernly.com

Okishima & Simmonds
okishimasimmonds.com

Old Harbor Distilling Co
oldharbordistilling.com

Olivine Atelier
shopolivine.com

One Eleven
oneelevenphotography.com

Papelline
etsy.com/uk/shop/papelline

Plush Events
instagram.com/plushevent

Produce Candles
producecandles.com

Rewined
rewinedcandles.com

Romy Colle
romycolle.com

Selencky Parsons
selenckyparsons.com

Smyth & Barry
smythandbarry.com

Stuart McMahon Garden Design
@Stu_mcmahon

The Future Kept
thefuturekept.com

The Medicine Garden
themedicinegarden.com

The Modern Dame
moderndame.com

The Transatlantic
the-transatlantic.com

Toni Edge Photography
toniedgephotography.com

Veris
veris-strategies.co.uk

Whoa Nelly
whoanellycatering.com

ARTWORK AND PHOTOGRAPHY CREDITS

All images ©Matt Pereira and styled by Fiona Humberstone unless otherwise stated.

2, 3: Produce Candles by Stitch Design Co, photography Sully Sullivan Photography; 6: Manuela Bertol by Braizen; 8, 9: Lucky Lab Coffee Co by Braizen, photography by Jen Dillender; 11: Geraldine Tan for Little Big Bell; 14, 15: Hannah Bergen by Stitch Design Co, photography Sully Sullivan Photography; 18: Unsplash; 19: Pretty Unexpected by Aline Bouma; Artichoke postcard image Whitney Neal for Lauren Ledbetter; 20: Unsplash; Pretty Unexpected by Aline Bouma; 22: Little Shop of Brands; 23: Stitch Design Co for Edmund's Oast, photography by Peter Frank Edwards; 25: Aline Bouma; 24: Jill Smith by Braizen, photography by Brooke Schwab; 28, 29: Okishima & Simmonds by Lauren Ledbetter; 30: Clare Nolan; 33, 34: Selencky Parsons for Given London; Flowers & Tea: Fiona Humberstone; 35: Loaf; 36: Selencky Parsons for Given London; 37: Loaf; 38: Finding Home by Braizen, photography by Erin Witkowski; 40: Jill Smith photographed by Brooke Schwab; 41: Little Shop of Brands; 42: Rowan Made; 43: The Future Kept; 46: Produce Candles by Stitch Design Co, photography by Sully Sullivan Photography; 54: Little Shop of Brands; 56: Clare Nolan; 59: Wire Rack, Loaf; 64: Seasonal Images, Fiona Humberstone except for White Roses and Frosted Succulents by Maddie Hatton and Apples by Aline Bouma; 66: Bluebells by Lisa Cox; 68, 69: One Eleven by Braizen, photography by One Eleven; 70: Beach by Aline Bouma, Peas and Friands, Maddie Hatton, Flowers, Fiona Humberstone Grasses, Unsplash; 72: Flowerona by Salted Ink Design Co, photography, Emily Quinton; 74: Fiona Humberstone; 76: Arthur Cottam by Tonik; 78: Blue Sky, Witch Hazel, Fiona Humberstone, Snowy Stream: Peter Gloyns, Pear: Maddie Hatton, Misty Valley, Lisa Cox, Snowflakes on Head, Aline Bouma; 80: Olivine Atelier by We Are Branch, photography Betsy Mobbs; 82: Death to the Stock Photo; 83: Commonplace by Rowan Made; 84, 85: Clare Nolan; 86, 87: Emily Quinton; 88: Whitney Neal photography for Lauren Ledbetter; 91: Mood board features Story Brand Logo by Lauren Ledbetter, Seven Hills logo by Meticulous Ink, Lovers, Seekers, Dreamers, Wanderers artwork by Studio 9 for The Call of Summer; 94: Fiona Humberstone; 95: Top right: features Arianna's Daily; bottom right, Belinda Love Lee; 101: Deathtothestockphoto; 99, 106, 108: Braizen photographed by Anne Almasy; 109: Caava Design for Whoa Nelly; 110, 111: edge images Braizen photographed by Anne Almasy; Medicine Garden logo by Topright Design; Bookishly logo by Nothing But Lovely; Mozell logo by Braizen; 113: Floral Theory logo by Julie Song Ink, Papelline and Grange Corner Farm logos by Minna May; Smyth & Barry & EnRoute Photography by Belinda Love Lee; Blush Photography by Grit and Wit; Veris & Career on Your Terms by Making Waves Creative; Haute Chefs, Commonplace Personal Goods & Nectar & Green by Rowan Made; Hotel deWindketel by Pretty Unexpected; Hero by Hero; Maras Creative by Jon King Design; The Transatlantic by Cocorinna; Lucends by Eva Black Design; The Future Kept by The Future Kept; The Modern Dame by Studio 9; 115: Romy Colle by Revival Designbüro; 117: Bare Blooms by Dilley & Jones, floral photography by Gemma Williams; 118: Aline Bouma by Pretty Unexpected; 121: Kate Whelan Events by Saffron Avenue; 122: I Heart Organizing by Saffron Avenue; 124: Pretty Unexpected by Aline Bouma; 125: Lenore Design by Salted Ink; 126: Stuart McMahon by Ditto, JC Lemon by Braizen; 130, 131: Jill Smith by Braizen; 132, 133: Chimpanas by Tonik; 134: Turquoise by Belinda Love Lee; Blue & Yellow Paint by Lauren Ledbetter; 136: Food photography and styling, Maddie Hatton; 139: Fiona Humberstone; 142: Little Shop of Brands; 147: Fiona Humberstone; 148: Bodoni Book, Fiona Humberstone; 149: Logo Sketches, Pinegate Road; 151: Medicinal Meal Plans by Buttercup Ink; 153: Toni Edge by Serafini Creative; 154: Mozell Films by Braizen; 154, 155: Braizen photographed by Anne Almasy; 158, 159: Old Harbor by Caava Design; 161: Rewined by Stitch Design Co; 163: Veris by Making Waves Creative; 165: Bayntun by Meticulous Ink; 166, 167: Allison Sosna Group by Serafini Creative; 168,169: Rewined by Stitch Design Co, photography by Sully Sullivan Photography; 170: Camera image, Death to the Stock Photo; 171: Joe & Patience by Caava Design; 173: Mozell Films by Braizen; 175: Career on Your Terms by Making Waves Creative; 176, 177: Plush Events by Grit & Wit; 180: Diana Marie Photography; 184: Produce Candles by Stitch Design Co, photography Sully Sullivan Photography; 186: Jill Smith by Braizen, photography by Brooke Schwab; 187: Amanda Lenhardt by Pinegate Road; 188, 189: Holli Thompson design/creative direction by Viewers Like You, photography by Chelsea Fullerton and Illustration by Very Marta; 190, 191: Lucky Lab Coffee Co by Braizen, photography by Jen Dillender; 192, 193: Northernly, Logo by Rae Ann Kelly, website design by Northernly, photography by Shay Cochrane; 195: Rewined by Stitch Design Co; 195: Nathalie Marguez Courtney by Belinda Love Lee; 196, 197: Whoa Nelly by Caava Design; 198: Diana Marie Photography by James Prunean; 199: Lucky Lab Coffee Co by Braizen, photography by Jen Dillender; 201: Mikaela Hamilton for Lauren Ledbetter; 208: Author portrait: Vicki Knights.

The publisher has made every effort to accurately gain permission from and credit all parties. Any errors or omissions will be corrected in a future print run.

ACKNOWLEDGEMENTS

Writing may well be a solitary pursuit, but producing a book is all about the teamwork. There are a huge number of people whose time, support and expertise have made this the book it is, and for that I'm immensely grateful.

Heartfelt thanks go to Jo Copestick, my editor, whose calm and reassuring tones and industry know-how have given me the much-needed confidence to make this crazy idea happen. Jane Means, thank you so much for introducing us in the first place. Enormous thanks to photographer fabuloso, Matt Pereira, who once again has pulled it out of the bag, dropped everything and created some wonderful images. Seriously Matt, you're the nuts.

The process in this book is the result of 15 years' experience; of trial and error; and of learning about what works, what doesn't, and why. None of this would have been possible without my clients, past and present, whose businesses have inspired, informed and shaped my work and the talented creatives I've had the pleasure of working alongside. Thank you.

I'm overwhelmingly, stupendously and simultaneously both grateful to and in awe of the featured businesses, photographers and creatives who have so generously shared their work and in doing so, created a visual feast. Work with them on your brand styling project - they are incredible!

Writing this book may have been a breeze, but the production has been quite a roller-coaster. Most often fun, but sometimes not, I would never have got through this without dear friends who have shared their thoughts, read proofs, challenged my ideas and provided much needed cheerleading services. There are far too many of you to name, I hope you know who you are. In particular I'd like to mention and give extra special thanks to Rona Wheeldon, Elizabeth Cairns, Clare Yarwood-White, Lisa Cox, Caroline Harrison, Julia Abab, Christina Grieve, Garet Tynan, Michelle Scott, Helen Kuhle and Helen & Dom Sharland. Thank you a million times over.

Thank you also to the companies who generously supplied props: Derwent Pencils, Fired Earth, Pantone, Serax and Dave at the Cedar Nursery in Cobham.

Last but by no means least, thank you and heaps of love to the people that mean the world to me: Poppy, Jasper, Ellie and Pete. Ellie and Jasper: having you bounce home from school every day asking me: 'How many pages today, Mummy?' or giving me your funny suggestions for photos to use has kept me going to the end. And Pete, the most hands-on dad I know. None of this would have been remotely possible without you. I love you.

207

ABOUT THE AUTHOR

Fiona Humberstone has been styling brands, creating websites and running workshops since 2000. An exacting Creative Director and commercially-minded entrepreneur, Fiona brings clarity and possibility to every project she works on.

Having founded, grown and sold one of the UK's most successful brand styling companies, Fiona now works as a freelance Creative Director for branding projects and consults for design agencies who want to sell more creative work.

Fiona partners with leading industry experts to run game-changing courses both online and around the world and is available for speaking engagements. Find out more at **fionahumberstone.com** and **thebrand-stylist.com**.

Also by Fiona Humberstone:

Exhibit! How to use Exhibitions to Grow Your Small Business